What Others Are S̶

ACEEE's Green Book

The Environmental Guide to Cars & Trucks

"...the country's preeminent guide to environmentally friendly passenger cars and trucks."

— JOHN O'DELL, *Los Angeles Times*

"The next time someone asks what one person can do … tell him or her to buy [ACEEE's] *Green Book*™. Just as the Kelley Blue Book is the definitive guide to auto prices, the *ACEEE's Green Book*™, updated annually, gives a comprehensive environmental impact statement for every passenger vehicle sold in America. It's far more than just a fuel economy guide."

— TOM HORTON, *Baltimore Sun*

"This handy guide rates cars by class and allows consumers to compare models based on emissions and fuel consumption."

— GRISTMAGAZINE.COM's "Car Talk" by Consumers Union

"If you want to get a picture of exactly what impact your vehicle has during its entire life cycle, *ACEEE's Green Book*™ is the place."

— TARA BAUKUS MELLO, thecarconnection.com

"Super-size sport/utility vehicles that should carry names like 'Leviathan' and 'Gigantor' continue to gain in popularity. But the same manufacturers that produce these vehicles are also designing cars and trucks that minimize harmful environmental effects. To learn what demands your vehicle makes on the planet, check [it] out."

— *BETTER HOMES AND GARDENS*

"The vast range of cars in the marketplace from relatively clean hybrids and electric cars to gas-guzzling behemoths shows why *ACEEE's Green Book*™ is so important. All too often clever marketing and deceptive awards confuse consumers looking for green cars. [This book] separates the contenders from the pretenders."

— DAN BECKER, Director, Sierra Club Global Warming and Energy Program

"...an extraordinary public service ... *ACEEE's Green Book*™ will change the way we buy cars...consumers now have the ability to make a real difference in the health of our fragile planet."
—JACK GILLIS, Director of Public Affairs, Consumer Federation of America and author of *The Ultimate Car Book*

"...uses a novel approach to provide comprehensive ratings of environmentally friendly and hazardous vehicles. Combining fuel-economy, tailpipe emissions and manufacturing impacts, the book assigns every vehicle a Green Score, which compares across classes, and a class ranking, which judges it alongside its peers."
— STEVE COHEN, *SKI Magazine*

"A Park School senior with an active conscience, abundant effrontery and a deficiency in prudence proposed last year that environmentally concerned students go up and down the car pool line asking SUV owners to buy more efficient vehicles ... [*ACEEE's Green Book*™] can help you protect the environment and protect yourself from zealous students."
— JOHN ROEMER, Upper School Librarian, The Park School, Baltimore, Maryland

"What's novel about *ACEEE's Green Book*™ is that it doesn't rely on the traditional miles-per-gallon rating to determine what's green. Instead the criteria are: Fuel costs per year...Health costs per year ... Tons of greenhouse gases emitted per year."
— MSNBC.com

"Good information is vital to helping consumers make environmentally smart choices. *ACEEE's Green Book*™ can help you make a wiser choice when you next buy a car or truck. It will help you find a cleaner, greener vehicle for the driving you can't avoid."
— MICHAEL REPLOGLE, Federal Transportation Director, Environmental Defense

"...practical buying advice, and a good primer on the eco-impacts of vehicles on global warming and public health."
— JOEL MAKOWER, Editor, *Green Business Letter*

"For more about 'buying green' and reducing car pollution, you can go online and visit the ACEEE's 'Green Cars' Web site at GreenerCars.com."
— THE COSTCO CONNECTION

"...truly valuable [web] site ... The site places a strong emphasis on how much energy efficiency can help the environment."

— *CHICAGO TRIBUNE*

"Only ACEEE's [*Green Book*™] provides complete and accessible information covering the many aspects of automotive environmental performance."

— *SOLAR TODAY*

"Unhealthy soot and smog, global warming, oil dependence — all of these problems are linked to our love affair with the automobile. *ACEEE's Green Book*™ gives consumers the information they need to make smart choices that do less harm to the environment."

— JOHN ADAMS, President, Natural Resources Defense Council

"Now there is no excuse for remaining ignorant of your auto's impact on the environment. If you are concerned about your lungs, air pollution, water pollution, and global warming, and want to do your part to curtail ever-increasing auto emissions, read [this book]."

— *AUDUBON NATURALIST NEWS*

"*ACEEE's Green Book*™ makes an important contribution to public awareness about motor vehicles. Use it when shopping for a new car!"

— JOAN CLAYBROOK, President, Public Citizen

"If you are about to purchase a ... car or truck, ...check out this book before you drive off the lot."

— South Coast Air Quality Managements District's *ADVISOR*

"Consumers are increasingly demanding environmental performance as well as horsepower from their automobiles. *ACEEE's Green Book*™ will help people pick cars that are easy on the environment and on the pocketbook when folks go to the gas pump."

—HANK DITTMAR, Campaign Director,
Surface Transportation Policy Project

"Don't go after your next vehicle without first consulting *ACEEE's Green Book*™!"

— *THE MIDWEST BOOK REVIEW'S* "Internet Bookwatch"

"If we're going to buy cars, we might as well buy the ones that are the most environmentally friendly. *ACEEE's Green Book*™ is the best resource available for helping us do that."

— *CO-OP AMERICA QUARTERLY*

"If you care about the environment and are about to buy a new vehicle, this is the book for you. [It] provides practical information to help you make a greener choice."

— HOWARD RIS, President, Union of Concerned Scientists

"This book is well done and is chock-full of meaningful, accessible information."

— Campaign on Auto Pollution's *GETTING THERE*

"If you insist on driving a car, check out *ACEEE's Green Book™*."

— Earth Island Institute's *JOURNAL*

"Even if you're not in the market for a new car, I can still recommend this guide if you're interested in quickly learning the basics of air pollution, climate change and greenhouse gas emissions. It's one of the best basic primers on all the various impacts of automobiles on the environment, how the industry is addressing much needed change, and how consumers can help."

— *SAN DIEGO EARTHWORKS*

ACEEE's Green Book™
The Environmental Guide to Cars and Trucks

MODEL YEAR 2002

ACEEE's Green Book™
The Environmental Guide to Cars and Trucks

MODEL YEAR 2002

by John DeCicco and James Kliesch

American Council for an Energy-Efficient Economy
Washington, D.C.
2002

ACEEE's Green Book™:
The Environmental Guide to Cars and Trucks—Model Year 2002

Published by the American Council for an Energy-Efficient Economy, 1001 Connecticut Avenue, N.W., Suite 801, Washington, D.C. 20036

Printed in the United States of America

www.GreenerCars.com

Written comments on this publication are welcome; send your comments to:

mail: Automotive Editor
         American Council for an Energy-Efficient Economy
         1001 Connecticut Avenue, N.W., Suite 801
         Washington, D.C. 20036-5525

e-mail: greenercars@aceee.org

Printed on recycled paper

Table of Contents

Acknowledgments xi

Introduction 1
   The Environmental Impacts of Automobiles 3

Buying Green 5
   Green Scores and Class Rankings 5
   How to Tell Which Emission Standard a Vehicle Meets 7

The Best of 2002 11
   The Top-Rated Models by Vehicle Class 13

Highlights of the Model Year 23
   Greener Choices 2002 25
   Greener Choices for Everyone 25
   The Top Scorers of 2002 26
   Greenest Vehicles of 2002 27
   Electric Vehicles 27
   Light Trucks—Most Still Score Poorly 30
   Meanest Vehicles for the Environment in 2002 31
   It's a Car. It's a Truck. It's a...Crossover Vehicle. 33
   What About Diesels? 34
   Bi- and Flex-Fuel Vehicles 34

Green by Design 37
   Greener Tech Today 38
   Earth-Friendlier Family Sedans 40
   Edging Toward Eco-Improved SUVs 42
   Hybrids are Happening 48
   Hybrid Electric Vehicles 49
   Greener Tech Tomorrow 57

Green Ratings for 2002 Vehicles 63
Sample Listing and Key to *ACEEE's Green Book*™ 64
Two Seaters 66
Subcompact Cars 68
Compact Cars 73
Small Wagons 80
Midsize Cars 82
Midsize Wagons 87
Large Cars 88
Minivans 90
Large Vans 92
Compact Pickups 94
Standard Pickups 97
Compact SUVs 99
Midsize SUVs 102
Large SUVs 107

Driving Green 111
Drive Carefully and Gently 111
Maintenance Tips 112
Take Advantage of "Commuter Choice" Programs 114

Automobiles and the Environment.....................117
Major Pollutants Associated with Automobiles 120
Pollution from a Typical New Car and Light Truck 121
Cars, Trucks, and Global Warming 126
Fuel Economy and Air Pollution 129
Efficiency and Safety 129

For Further Information 133

Appendix: How the Ratings Are Calculated 137

List of Acronyms 141

Alphabetical Vehicle Index 143

Bibliography 149

About the Authors 151

Acknowledgments

The authors would like to acknowledge the many individuals whose advice and suggestions helped us produce this publication. For technical comments and other assistance, we thank Dave Brzezinski, Dan Harrison, John Koupal, Seung Park, and Lisa Snapp of the U.S. Environmental Protection Agency (with special gratitude to Seung Park for his assistance in accessing the data used to prepare the guide), as well as Duc Nguyen and his staff at the California Air Resources Board. We are also grateful to Mark Delucchi, John German, David Greene, Charles Griffith, Dave Hermance, Darin Johnson, Ben Knight, Walt Kreucher, Kevin Mills, Carl Nash, Prabhakar Patil, David Rodgers, and Michael Wang for their valuable input. We further thank the many automaker representatives for providing data, comments, and photographs.

At ACEEE, we thank Therese Langer, Daniel Williams, and Toru Kubo for their help in suggesting improvements, providing technical assistance, and editing; we thank Glee Murray and Susan Ziff for production, and Renee Nida for editing and proofreading. Additional thanks are given to Chuck Myers for design and layout. We are grateful for support of technical research and analytic work by the U.S. Department of Energy's Office of Transportation Technologies. For supporting the publication of *ACEEE's Green Book*™, we express our gratitude to The Energy Foundation and the Joyce Foundation.

Introduction

Many considerations go into buying a new car or light truck. You'll consider price, styling, comfort, performance, safety, reliability, and of course, how well the vehicle will serve your needs. The decision comes down to cost versus value: how much you are willing to pay for the features you want to get. But the costs of car use go beyond what's on the sticker and what you'll spend on fuel and repairs. The toll that cars and trucks take on the environment is often hidden but always very real. This toll includes unhealthy air pollution, oil spills and fouling of water supplies, damage to habitats, and global climate disruption. If you care about the environment, then what you value goes beyond performance or styling and the options featured in the showroom.

ACEEE's Green Book™ helps you choose a greener vehicle, one that is cleaner and more fuel-efficient, minimizing harm to the environment while meeting your transportation needs.

■ For families with several vehicles, the pollution from their cars, vans, sport utilities, and pickup trucks is often greater than that from electricity and heating fuel use, waste disposal, and other household activities.

■ Automobile pollution can be more dangerous than similar amounts of pollution from large sources such as power plants, since car and truck emissions are quite literally "in your face" where we live, work, shop, and play.

■ Much more will have to be done to clean up cars and light trucks in order to avoid pollution alerts and bring air quality up to more healthful levels in many U.S. cities and regions.

Car and truck pollution not only harms our health in the present, but also contributes to global warming, bringing greater problems in years to come. A watchword of environmentalism is the concept of "sustainability." An action is sustainable if it serves our needs today without jeopardizing the ability of future generations (our children and grandchildren) to meet their needs. The large amount of energy consumed and pollution produced by cars and trucks is the biggest reason our transportation system is not sustainable.

1

> Carbon dioxide (CO_2) is the most important greenhouse gas (GHG), referring to substances that trap heat in the earth's atmosphere and cause global warming. The largest portion of harmful GHG emissions is the CO_2 released from burning fossil fuels: oil, coal, and natural gas.

Carbon dioxide emissions from the consumption of gasoline, diesel, and other fossil fuels are the principal cause of global warming, which brings health and economic risks from climate change.

- The United States is the world's largest emitter of CO_2 and our emissions are still rising steadily. It will take decades before China and other rapidly growing economies reach our levels of CO_2 pollution per person.

- American cars and light trucks alone account for more fossil fuel CO_2 emissions than the total nationwide emissions of all but three other countries in the world.

- Buying more fuel-efficient cars and light trucks is one of the single biggest steps we can take to reduce global warming.

Making motor vehicles cleaner and more efficient is an important step toward sustainable transportation. A large part of this task is up to automakers, but choosing a greener vehicle is a step you can take that will head us in the right direction.

Today's automobiles—this book's general term for cars, pickup trucks, station wagons, minivans, sport utilities, and other personal motor vehicles—are made much cleaner than those of a generation ago. Nevertheless, they remain among the largest causes of environmental damage. Environmental impacts start when automobiles are made, continue throughout their life on the road, and don't end even when the vehicles are scrapped, since waste disposal creates pollution, too.

Even the cleanest and most efficient vehicle on the market today still pollutes the air and otherwise damages the environment. A number of air pollutants are associated with automobiles:

- Fine airborne particulate matter (PM) causes lung trouble— shortness of breath, worsening of respiratory diseases and heart conditions, lung damage, and cancer.

- Nitrogen oxides (NO_x) aggravate respiratory problems, both directly and indirectly, by forming PM and smog; NO_x also causes acid rain and damages aquatic environments.

The Environmental Impacts of Automobiles

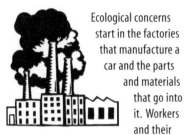

Ecological concerns start in the factories that manufacture a car and the parts and materials that go into it. Workers and their communities are exposed to air and water pollution, toxins, and other hazards.

Gasoline and diesel fuel are poisonous to humans, plants and animals, and their fumes are toxic. Air and water pollution occur at oil wells, refineries, and filling stations and when petroleum products are transported by ship, pipeline, and truck. The more fuel we burn, the greater these impacts.

Much of the pollution from today's average automobile is in the exhaust. Government regulations prevent properly functioning new cars from polluting nearly as much as they did in the past. But personal vehicles still cause smog, toxics, and invisible but deadly fine particles that foul the air.

Whether in a crash or by old age, an automobile and its parts eventually get scrapped. Some components, including most of the steel, are recycled, but vehicle disposal still contaminates the air, water, and land.

Consumption of gasoline, diesel, and other petroleum products is the largest source of the greenhouse gas emissions that cause global warming. The risks from this growing form of planet pollution include increased storms, droughts, and heat waves, spread of tropical diseases, rising sea levels, coastal flooding, and damage to agriculture, the economy, and ecosystems.

> A gallon of gasoline weighs just over 6 pounds. When burned, the carbon in it combines with oxygen from the air to produce 19 pounds of CO_2. But counting the energy that went into making and distributing the fuel, the total global warming impact equals 28 pounds of CO_2 emissions per gallon.

- Sulfur dioxide (SO_2) also irritates the lungs, and it contributes to forming PM as well as acid rain.

- Hydrocarbons (HC) are volatile organic compounds that cause smog and are toxic and carcinogenic.

- Carbon monoxide (CO) is a poisonous gas that impairs the flow of oxygen to the brain and other parts of the body.

- Carbon dioxide (CO_2) is not normally harmful, but the huge amount of CO_2 released by burning gasoline and other fossil fuels causes global warming.

Understanding the polluting effects of automobiles can help one appreciate the importance of considering a vehicle's greenness (or lack of greenness) when it comes time to purchase one. More information can be found later in this book, under "Automobiles and the Environment," and online at GreenerCars.com.

Greener Transport Also Means Reducing Driving

A vehicle's greenness depends not only on its design, but also on how it is used. A car is greener when it's carrying two people rather than one and it's greener still with three. And it's greenest of all if left at home when there's a cleaner way to go: by foot or by bicycle, by bus or by train, and even by wire (telecommuting or videoconferencing). Consider your opportunities to reduce car use when practical, by walking or biking for short trips, ridesharing, and combining several errands into one trip.

Our options for getting to work or school, shopping or recreation, conducting business, and visiting family or friends depend very much on where we live. Choosing where you live for its walkability and convenience to work, school, or transit—what planners call location efficiency—is a key way to reduce your need for driving. In some areas, people find it surprisingly easy to do without a car at all.

Commuters may be eligible for benefits from their employers for transit or carpooling, or can receive cash by simply walking, biking, or telecommuting. See details on "Commuter Choice" programs on page 114.

Buying Green

*A*CEEE's *Green Book™* will help you select the vehicle that is most friendly to the planet while meeting your transportation needs. Based on official emissions and fuel-economy tests, and other specifications reported by auto manufacturers, we calculate a Green Score for each car, van, pickup, and sport utility on the market. The Green Score falls on a scale of zero to 100. A higher score implies a greener car, meaning a vehicle having a lower environmental impact.

Green Scores and Class Rankings

In our tables, vehicles are grouped together by class (that is, the type or body style, such as midsize car, minivan, standard pickup, and so on). To summarize our ratings and make it easy to find the top-rated vehicles, we use five symbols based on a model's rank within its class. No vehicle gets a Superior (✔) rating if its Green Score is worse than the overall average of all vehicles offered this model year, even if it ranks among the best in its class. Look for models with a check mark (✔), or next best, an upward triangle (▲), to find those that have the greenest scores.

To highlight the most planet-friendly new cars and trucks, the next section of the *Green Book* features "The Best of 2002." It lists the vehicles having the highest Green Scores in each class. The easiest way to buy green is to select a vehicle from the "Best of 2002" list.

Starting on page 63, our Green Ratings master table details each vehicle's emissions standard, fuel economy, fuel costs, health effects, CO_2 emissions, and overall environmental impact, along with its Green Score and Class Ranking. If you have identified a set of models to consider, you can look them up in this table to comparison shop with the environment in mind.

For most consumers, the Green Score and Class Ranking provide

Class Ranking Symbols	
✔	Superior
▲	Above Average
○	Average
▽	Below Average
✖	Inferior
Indicate a vehicle's environmental performance relative to others in its class.	

Different Versions of a Model Have Different Green Scores

Nearly all models come in different configurations, meaning different choices of engine, transmission, and other major options. A model may also be available in versions that meet different emissions standards or run on alternative fuels. To match a model in the show room with a listing in the *Green Book*, first match its emissions standard. Some cars will have a special label denoting "ULEV," for example. Then match its city and highway fuel economy ratings, which vary with engine size and transmission type.

---

a good indication of a car's environmental performance. We explain the factors behind the Green Score in the appendix, "How the Ratings Are Calculated." In general, a vehicle is greener if it is cleaner (less air pollution) or more fuel efficient (resulting in lower energy consumption and CO_2 emissions).

All new vehicles for sale in the United States are certified to meet either Federal emissions standards, set by the U.S. Environmental Protection Agency (EPA), or California standards, set by the California Air Resources Board (CARB). These exhaust emissions standards limit the amounts of key pollutants coming from a vehicle's tailpipe and leaks in its fuel system. California has a set of standards that are progressively more stringent by pollutant. The principal tailpipe standards applicable to new vehicles are:

Tier 1   the prevailing Federal (EPA) standard.

Tier 1-D the Federal diesel standard; permits higher NO_x emissions.

HDT   Heavy Duty Truck, the weakest standard for light trucks.

TLEV   Transitional Low-Emission Vehicle, the weakest California standard.

LEV   Low-Emission Vehicle, an intermediate California standard about twice as stringent as Tier 1.

ULEV   Ultra-Low-Emission Vehicle, a stronger California standard emphasizing very low HC emissions.

SULEV   Super-Ultra-Low-Emission Vehicle, a California standard even tighter than ULEV including much lower NO_x emissions and more durable control systems.

ZEV   Zero-Emission Vehicle, a California standard prohibiting any tailpipe emissions.

This year, most cars and light trucks available nationwide meet one of the cleaner, low-emission standards, particularly the LEV standard. However, some ULEVs and most SULEVs—representing the cleanest vehicles, or cleanest versions of models certified to multiple standards—are only available in California or other states that have adopted California rules. We give such restricted-availability vehicles shaded listings in our tables, to distinguish them from models that are more widely available.

The levels of pollution permitted under each standard depend on the vehicle type. Many light trucks have weaker standards than cars.

How to Tell Which Emission Standard a Vehicle Meets

This year, most models are available nationally in one of the low-emission vehicle (LEV-type) standards, such as LEV or ULEV. These stricter tailpipe limits are required in California, Massachusetts, New York, Vermont, and Maine. In other states, some models may still only meet the minimum Federal standards. Regardless of where you live, identifying a vehicle's emission standard is easy.

Emissions Label

Many automakers now list their cars' and trucks' emission standards under the "Vehicle Specs" sections of their websites. Some vehicles now have stickers or window decals identifying the certification level. All vehicles, however, have a mandatory under-the-hood label that identifies the emission standard—so while you're standing on the dealer's lot, just pop

1 VEHICLE EMISSION CONTROL INFORMATION

2 ENGINE FAMILY 2HNXV01.7NA5
DISPLACEMENT 1.7L
OBD II CERTIFIED

THIS VEHICLE CONFORMS TO U.S. EPA NLEV AND CALIFORNIA REGULATIONS APPLICABLE TO 2002 MODEL YEAR NEW ULEV PASSENGER CARS.

motor co, inc.

REFER TO SERVICE MANUAL FOR ADDITIONAL INFORMATION

3 TUNE UP CONDITIONS: NORMAL OPERATING ENGINE TEMPERATURE ACCESSORIES OFF, COOLING FAN OFF, TRANSMISSION IN NEUTRAL.

EXHAUST EMISSION STANDARDS CATEGORY
CERTIFICATION NLEV, ULEV
TEST FUEL: EPA UNLEADED GASOLINE

4 SPARK PLUG
TYPE NGK BPR6ES-11
GAP 1.1mm

CATALYST

2HNXV01.7NA5

1 Engine family number
2 Manufacturer identification
3 Emissions standard identification
4 Tune-up information

HOW EMISSIONS STANDARDS STACK UP

For any given standard, most minivans, pickups, and SUVs pollute more than sedans, coupes, or wagons.

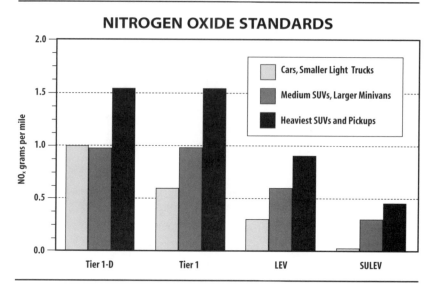

NITROGEN OXIDE STANDARDS

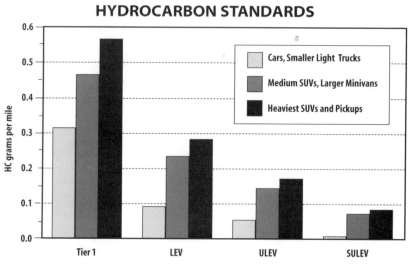

HYDROCARBON STANDARDS

Different types of vehicles are required to meet different levels of pollution control for any given standard. Most light trucks are allowed higher emissions than cars for any given standard. Tier 1 is the current Federal standard set by EPA; Tier 1-D is the weaker version that allows higher NO$_x$ emissions for disel engines. Not all standards are shown here; see page 6 for definitions.

Green Buyer Alert

The pollution coming from a vehicle depends on the standard it meets, how well its emissions controls work, how it is driven and maintained, fuel consumption, and fuel quality. Vans, pickup trucks, and sport utilities are classified by the government as light trucks, and so have less stringent emissions and fuel economy standards than passenger cars. As a result, the average light truck pollutes more than the average car (see the graphic comparison on page 121). Some of the heaviest light trucks, such as large sport utilities, are exempt from passenger vehicle regulations, and are among the most polluting of personal vehicles.

There are other standards not listed above, and new standards of increasing stringency are being issued by EPA and CARB. Each model's precise emissions standard is reflected in its Green Score and Class Ranking.

Automakers also rate their vehicles for fuel economy (miles per gallon—MPG) according to standard EPA tests of simulated city and highway driving. Unlike emissions standards, the fuel economy standards apply to manufacturers, rather than to individual vehicles. A manufacturer can sell models of varying fuel economy so long as their average fuel economy meets the standard. Light trucks (pickups, vans, and sport utilities) have a lower standard than passenger cars and station wagons. A new vehicle's sales sticker shows its city and highway MPG ratings; check these sticker MPG values to help you match a vehicle on the lot to a model listed in the *Green Book*.

Higher fuel economy means lower fuel consumption, savings on fuel costs, and reduced global warming emissions. Even in new vehicles, tailpipe standards don't fully control pollution in real-world driving conditions and don't capture the pollution effects related to the amount of fuel consumed. Therefore, among models meeting a given tailpipe emissions standard, higher fuel economy means lower total emissions of other pollutants as well.

Depending on where you live and how you use the vehicle, you may want to give greater or lesser importance to some factors over others. For this reason, our master table also provides details on a vehicle's health impacts, its global warming impacts, and its likely fuel costs. Buyers in urban areas, particularly areas with air quality problems, should emphasize models that meet tighter tailpipe standards, such as the California LEV or ULEV standards noted above.

The Best of 2002

The easiest way to choose a clean and efficient vehicle is to use this section of the *Green Book*, which lists the greenest models in each class. For instance, if you are in the market for a midsize sport utility vehicle, look under Midsize SUVs to find the top-rated models. You might also find a greener score among models with similar capabilities. Some SUV shoppers might want to check out Minivans or Midsize Wagons, for example.

The best scoring cars and trucks are those that meet one of the stricter low-emission vehicle standards (LEV, ULEV, and so on—see page 6 for descriptions). Many models are now available nationwide in one of these LEV-type standards. If you live in California, Massachusetts, New York, Vermont, or Maine—or in some sales regions near these four Northeastern states—then LEVs and even ULEVs are widely available. These five "Clean Car States" have adopted California's more stringent motor vehicle pollution control rules. However, the cleanest gasoline vehicles—some of those earning the status of a Super-Ultra-Low-Emission Vehicle (SULEV)—may be available only in California, since they require clean, low-sulfur gasoline to operate properly.

The Toyota Prius—a fuel-efficient gasoline-electric hybrid car—carries a SULEV rating in California, but ULEV elsewhere. Even

---

New Vehicles Aren't As Clean As You Think

Automakers sometimes claim that their new cars are "96 percent cleaner" than those of decades past. This statement isn't always true. Just because a new car or truck meets the new tailpipe standards doesn't mean that its pollution is adequately regulated. Actual emissions may average as much as double the standard levels. Automakers' claims are based on laboratory tests that may have a poor relation to typical driving. After all, what counts for our health is the air we breathe in real-world traffic, not in a laboratory with carefully controlled conditions. Our Green Scores account for this discrepancy between lab tests and real-world driving. This year, EPA is continuing to phase in more realistic test requirements that will reduce some of this excess tailpipe pollution.

though the emissions control technology on the vehicle is the same, Toyota cannot certify that the vehicle will achieve super-ultra-low emissions in states where dirtier gasoline is still permitted.

Some automakers have begun labeling their low-emission vehicles with a special sticker or decal, but in other cases you may have to examine the "fine print" on the main window sticker or look under the hood as described earlier on page 7. In any case, the best bet is to ask your dealer for the cleanest available versions of the models you are considering. Asking for greener cars and trucks sends an important message to dealers and automakers, encouraging them to offer a wider selection of environmentally friendly models.

In this "Best of 2002" section, we list models with automatic transmissions separately from those with manual transmissions. For some vehicle classes, no manuals are listed because they are unavailable or rare. Also, this table lists only the greener versions of a given make and model, not all of its configurations. See the *Green Book* master tables starting on page 63 for complete information.

Employing a special VTEC-E engine and an optional continuously variable transmission, Honda's sporty Civic HX is the fuel economy leader among subcompact cars.

Photo: American Honda Motor Co., Inc.

The Top-Rated Models by Vehicle Class

	Specifications*	Emission Standard	Fuel Economy City	Fuel Economy Hwy	Green Score	Class Ranking
TWO SEATERS						
AUTOMATICS						
HONDA INSIGHT	1.0L 3, auto CVT	SULEV	57	56	**57**	✔
MAZDA MX-5 MIATA	1.8L 4, auto [P]	LEV	22	28	**30**	▲
MANUALS						
HONDA INSIGHT	1.0L 3, manual	ULEV	61	68	**54**	✔
TOYOTA MR2	1.8L 4, manual	LEV	25	30	**33**	▲
SUBCOMPACT CARS						
AUTOMATICS						
HONDA CIVIC HX	1.7L 4, auto CVT	ULEV	35	40	**41**	✔
MITSUBISHI MIRAGE	1.5L 4, auto	LEV	28	35	**36**	▲
SUZUKI ESTEEM	1.6L 4, auto	LEV	27	34	**35**	▲
SATURN SC	1.9L 4, auto	LEV	26	36	**35**	▲
MANUALS						
HONDA CIVIC HX	1.7L 4, manual	ULEV	36	44	**42**	✔
MITSUBISHI MIRAGE	1.5L 4, manual	LEV	32	39	**39**	✔
SATURN SC	1.9L 4, manual	LEV	28	40	**37**	✔
SUZUKI ESTEEM	1.8L 4, manual	LEV	28	35	**36**	▲

The specifications include engine displacement in liters (L), number of cylinders, transmission type, and fuel type (e.g., P for premium); see the key on pages 64-65 for further details.

Toyota's hybrid-electric Prius uses advanced technologies to become the year's greenest gasoline-powered family sedan.

Photo: Toyota Motor Sales, U.S.A.

Specifications*	Emission Standard	Fuel Economy City	Fuel Economy Hwy	Green Score	Class Ranking

COMPACT CARS

AUTOMATICS

HONDA CIVIC GX	1.7L 4, auto CVT [CNG]²	SULEV	30	34	**52**	✔
TOYOTA PRIUS	1.5L 4, auto CVT	SULEV	52	45	**51**	✔
NISSAN SENTRA CA	1.8L 4, auto	SULEV	27	33	**40**	✔
HONDA CIVIC	1.7L 4, auto	ULEV	31	38	**39**	✔
TOYOTA ECHO	1.5L 4, auto	LEV	32	38	**39**	▲
CHEVROLET PRIZM†	1.8L 4, auto	LEV	30	40	**38**	▲
TOYOTA COROLLA†	1.8L 4, auto	LEV	30	39	**37**	▲

MANUALS

TOYOTA ECHO	1.5L 4, manual	LEV	34	41	**41**	✔
HONDA CIVIC	1.7L 4, manual	ULEV	33	39	**40**	✔
TOYOTA COROLLA†	1.8L 4, manual	LEV	32	41	**39**	▲
CHEVROLET PRIZM†	1.8L 4, manual	LEV	32	41	**39**	▲
SATURN SL	1.9L 4, manual	LEV	29	40	**38**	▲
NISSAN SENTRA	1.8L 4, manual	ULEV	27	35	**37**	▲
FORD FOCUS	2.0L 4, manual	ULEV	28	36	**37**	▲

* The specifications include engine displacement in liters (L), number of cylinders, transmission type, and fuel type (e.g., P for premium); see the key on pages 64-65 for further details.

† These vehicles are twins—the same base model carrying different names.

² Compressed natural gas (CNG) fuel economy is given as gasoline-equivalent MPG.

An efficient 2.2-liter engine and nationally available ultra-low emissions help propel the Saturn L100/200 to one of the top midsize car slots.

Photo: General Motors Corporation and Wieck Photo DataBase, Inc.

	Specifications*	Emission Standard	Fuel Economy City	Fuel Economy Hwy	Green Score	Class Ranking
SMALL WAGONS						
AUTOMATICS						
SUZUKI ESTEEM WAGON	1.6L 4, auto	LEV	26	33	**34**	✔
DAEWOO NUBIRA WAGON	2.0L 4, auto	LEV	22	31	**30**	▲
VOLKSWAGEN JETTA WAGON	2.0L 4, auto	ULEV	22	29	**30**	▲
MANUALS						
SUZUKI ESTEEM WAGON	1.8L 4, manual	LEV	27	34	**35**	✔
VOLKSWAGEN JETTA WAGON	2.0L 4, manual	ULEV	24	31	**32**	▲
DAEWOO NUBIRA WAGON	2.0L 4, manual	LEV	22	31	**31**	▲
MIDSIZE CARS						
AUTOMATICS						
HONDA ACCORD	2.3L 4, auto	SULEV	23	30	**34**	✔
SATURN L100/200	2.2L 4, auto	ULEV	24	33	**33**	✔
TOYOTA CAMRY	2.4L 4, auto	ULEV	23	32	**32**	▲
HONDA ACCORD	2.3L 4, auto	ULEV	23	30	**31**	▲
NISSAN ALTIMA	2.5L 4, auto	ULEV	23	29	**31**	▲
MAZDA 626	2.0L 4, auto	ULEV	22	28	**31**	▲

Best-in-class fuel economy, coupled with ULEV or LEV tailpipe emissions, give Ford's Focus Wagon top honors among midsize wagons. *Photo: Ford Motor Company and Wieck Photo DataBase, Inc.*

	Specifications*	Emission Standard	Fuel Economy City	Fuel Economy Hwy	Green Score	Class Ranking
MIDSIZE CARS (cont.)						
MANUALS						
MAZDA 626	2.0L 4, manual	ULEV	26	32	**35**	✔
SATURN L100/200	2.2L 4, manual	ULEV	25	33	**34**	✔
HONDA ACCORD	2.3L 4, manual	ULEV	26	32	**33**	✔
TOYOTA CAMRY	2.4L 4, manual	ULEV	24	33	**33**	✔
MIDSIZE WAGONS						
AUTOMATICS						
FORD FOCUS WAGON	2.0L 4, auto	ULEV	26	32	**34**	▲
SATURN LW200	2.2L 4, auto	ULEV	24	33	**32**	▲
VOLKSWAGEN PASSAT WAGON	1.8L 4, auto stk [P]	ULEV	21	30	**30**	▲
VOLVO V70	2.4L 5, auto [P]	ULEV	21	28	**29**	○
MANUALS						
FORD FOCUS WAGON	2.0L 4, manual	LEV	28	36	**35**	✔
SATURN LW200	2.2L 4, manual	ULEV	24	32	**32**	▲
VOLKSWAGEN PASSAT WAGON	1.8L 4, manual [P]	ULEV	22	31	**31**	▲
VOLVO V70	2.4L 5, manual [P]	ULEV	21	28	**29**	○

For the second year in a row, the ULEV-certified Chevrolet Venture (along with its twins, the Oldsmobile Silhouette and Pontiac Montana) takes the crown as the greenest minivan of the year. *Photo: General Motors Corporation and Wieck Photo DataBase, Inc.*

	Specifications*	Emission Standard	Fuel Economy City	Hwy	Green Score	Class Ranking
LARGE CARS						
AUTOMATICS						
FORD CROWN VICTORIA	4.6L 8, auto [CNG]²	ULEV	15	22	**32**	✔
CHEVROLET IMPALA	3.4L 6, auto	LEV	21	32	**29**	✔
TOYOTA AVALON	3.0L 6, auto	LEV	21	29	**29**	✔
MINIVANS						
AUTOMATICS						
CHEVROLET VENTURE††	3.4L 6, auto	ULEV	19	26	**25**	✔
OLDSMOBILE SILHOUETTE††	3.4L 6, auto	ULEV	19	26	**25**	✔
PONTIAC MONTANA††	3.4L 6, auto	ULEV	19	26	**25**	✔
CHRYSLER VOYAGER†	2.4L 4, auto	LEV	19	24	**24**	▲
DODGE CARAVAN†	2.4L 4, auto	LEV	19	24	**24**	▲
TOYOTA SIENNA	3.0L 6, auto	LEV	19	24	**23**	▲

The specifications include engine displacement in liters (L), number of cylinders, transmission type, and fuel type (e.g., P for premium); see the key on pages 64-65 for further details.

² *Compressed natural gas (CNG) fuel economy is given as gasoline-equivalent MPG.*

† *These vehicles are twins—the same base model carrying different names.*

†† *These vehicles are triplets—the same base model carrying different names.*

	Specifications*	Emission Standard	Fuel Economy City	Hwy	Green Score	Class Ranking

LARGE VANS

AUTOMATICS

	Specifications*	Emission Standard	City	Hwy	Green Score	Class Ranking
DODGE RAM VAN 2500	5.2L 8, auto [CNG] [2]	SULEV	13	15	**24**	✔
DODGE RAM WAGON 2500	5.2L 8, auto [CNG] [2]	SULEV	13	15	**23**	✔
FORD E-250 ECONOLINE	5.4L 8, auto [CNG] [2]	SULEV	11	14	**20**	▲
VOLKSWAGEN EUROVAN	2.8L 6, auto	TLEV	17	20	**18**	▲
FORD E-150 ECONOLINE	4.6L 8, auto	LEV	15	20	**17**	○
CHEVROLET G1500/2500 VAN	4.3L 6, auto	LEV	15	18	**17**	○
GMC G1500/2500 SAVANA						
(CARGO)	4.3L 6, auto	LEV	15	18	**17**	○

COMPACT PICKUPS

AUTOMATICS

	Specifications*	Emission Standard	City	Hwy	Green Score	Class Ranking
FORD RANGER	Electric [1]	ZEV	2.9	2.9	**34**	✔
TOYOTA TACOMA	2.4L 4, auto	LEV	22	25	**28**	▲
FORD RANGER [†]	2.3L 4, auto	LEV	21	25	**26**	▲
MAZDA B2300 [†]	2.3L 4, auto	LEV	21	25	**26**	▲
NISSAN FRONTIER	2.4L 4, auto	LEV	20	23	**25**	▲
CHEVROLET S-10 [††]	2.2L 4, auto	LEV	19	25	**25**	▲
GMC SONOMA [††]	2.2L 4, auto	LEV	19	25	**25**	▲
ISUZU HOMBRE [††]	2.2L 4, auto	LEV	19	25	**25**	▲

MANUALS

	Specifications*	Emission Standard	City	Hwy	Green Score	Class Ranking
FORD RANGER [†]	2.3L 4, manual	LEV	24	28	**29**	✔
MAZDA B2300 [†]	2.3L 4, manual	LEV	24	28	**29**	✔
TOYOTA TACOMA	2.4L 4, manual	LEV	22	27	**29**	✔
CHEVROLET S-10 [††]	2.2L 4, manual	LEV	22	28	**28**	▲
GMC SONOMA [††]	2.2L 4, manual	LEV	22	28	**28**	▲
ISUZU HOMBRE [††]	2.2L 4, manual	LEV	22	28	**28**	▲
NISSAN FRONTIER	2.4L 4, manual	LEV	22	25	**28**	▲

* The specifications include engine displacement in liters (L), number of cylinders, transmission type, and fuel type (e.g., P for premium); see the key on pages 64-65 for further details.

[1] Electric vehicle fuel economy is given in miles per kilowatt-hour (mi/kWh).

[2] Compressed natural gas (CNG) fuel economy is given as gasoline-equivalent MPG.

[†] These vehicles are twins—the same base model carrying different names.

[††] These vehicles are triplets—the same base model carrying different names.

With improved engines and pollution control technology, the Ford F-150 pickups meet LEV and even ULEV standards nationwide. The 4.2-liter V-6, 2-wheel drive models make our "Best of 2002" list. For fleets with access to natural gas, Ford's CNG pickups meet ULEV and SULEV standards and score even better on our green rating scale.

Ford Motor Company and Wieck Photo DataBase, Inc.

	Specifications*	Emission Standard	Fuel Economy City	Hwy	Green Score	Class Ranking
STANDARD PICKUPS						
AUTOMATICS						
FORD F-150	5.4L 8, auto [CNG] [2]	SULEV	12	16	**23**	✔
FORD F-150	5.4L 8, auto [CNG] [2]	ULEV	12	16	**20**	▲
FORD F-150	4.2L 6, auto	ULEV	16	20	**20**	▲
TOYOTA TUNDRA	3.4L 6, auto	LEV	16	19	**20**	▲
MANUALS						
FORD F-150	4.2L 6, manual	ULEV	17	21	**21**	▲
TOYOTA TUNDRA	3.4L 6, manual	LEV	16	19	**20**	▲
GMC SIERRA C1500	4.8L 8, manual	LEV	16	20	**19**	▲
COMPACT SUVs						
AUTOMATICS						
TOYOTA RAV4	Electric [1]	ZEV	3.7	2.9	**52**	✔
TOYOTA RAV4	2.0L 4, auto	LEV	24	29	**31**	✔
CHEVROLET TRACKER CONVERTIBLE	2.0L 4, auto	LEV	23	26	**29**	▲
CHEVROLET TRACKER HARDTOP	2.0L 4, auto	LEV	23	26	**29**	▲
SATURN VUE	2.2L 4, auto CVT	ULEV	22	28	**29**	▲
HONDA CR-V	2.4L 4, auto	LEV	23	28	**29**	▲

The 2-wheel drive version of Buick's all-new Rendezvous is one of the top-scoring midsize SUVs of the year. All-wheel drive versions of the vehicle also score above average for its class.

Photo: General Motors Corporation and Wieck Photo DataBase, Inc.

	Specifications*	Emission Standard	Fuel Economy City	Fuel Economy Hwy	Green Score	Class Ranking
COMPACT SUVs (cont.)						
MANUALS						
TOYOTA RAV4	2.0L 4, manual	LEV	25	31	**32**	✔
CHEVROLET TRACKER CONVERTIBLE	2.0L 4, manual	LEV	23	26	**29**	▲
CHEVROLET TRACKER HARDTOP	2.0L 4, manual	LEV	23	26	**29**	▲
SUZUKI VITARA 2-DOOR	2.0L 4, manual	LEV	23	26	**29**	▲
MIDSIZE SUVs						
AUTOMATICS						
TOYOTA HIGHLANDER	2.4L 4, auto	LEV	22	27	**26**	✔
BUICK RENDEZVOUS†	3.4L 6, auto	ULEV	19	26	**25**	✔
PONTIAC AZTEK†	3.4L 6, auto	ULEV	19	26	**25**	✔
TOYOTA HIGHLANDER	3.0L 6, auto	LEV	19	23	**23**	▲
MITSUBISHI MONTERO SPORT	3.0L 6, auto	LEV	18	22	**22**	▲
ACURA MDX	3.5L 6, auto 4wd [P]	ULEV	17	23	**22**	▲

*The specifications include engine displacement in liters (L), number of cylinders, transmission type, and fuel type (e.g., P for premium); see the key on pages 64-65 for further details.
† These vehicles are twins—the same base model carrying different names.

	Specifications*	Emission Standard	Fuel Economy City	Fuel Economy Hwy	Green Score	Class Ranking
MIDSIZE SUVs (cont.)						
MANUALS						
NISSAN XTERRA	2.4L 4, manual	LEV	19	24	**23**	▲
ISUZU RODEO	2.2L 4, manual	LEV	19	23	**23**	▲
FORD EXPLORER SPORT	4.0L 6, manual	LEV	17	22	**21**	▲
LARGE SUVs						
AUTOMATICS						
FORD EXPEDITION	4.6L 8, auto	LEV	15	20	**17**	▲
CHEVROLET TAHOE C1500 †	4.8L 8, auto	LEV	15	19	**16**	▲
GMC YUKON C1500 †	4.8L 8, auto	LEV	15	19	**16**	▲

Highlights of the Model Year

Model year 2002 brings continuing progress with vehicle designs that cut smog-forming tailpipe pollution, but also continuing stagnation of the overall fuel efficiency in the new car and light truck market. Hope for the future is represented by hybrid-electric vehicles, which are the most exiting "green" products now in automotive showrooms. This next-generation technology saw its U.S. debut with the arrival of the Honda Insight in 2000 and the Toyota Prius for model year 2001. As this year's *Green Book* goes to press, we are anticipating the introduction of a hybrid-electric version of the Honda Civic, soon to be available as an early model year 2003 car.

In spite of these promising developments, on balance the car and truck market is still headed down a road of environmental harm. As fuel economy continues to decline, oil dependence and global warming pollution continue to climb. Each new large SUV cruising the streets causes 50 percent more climate-threatening carbon dioxide (CO_2) emissions than the average vehicle already on the road. The top-scoring Honda Insight cuts CO_2 emissions by over 40 percent compared to similarly sized cars. But small cars are already more efficient and therefore produce less CO_2 than average. Compared to the standard Civic Hatchback, for instance, the Insight decreases CO_2 emissions by 2 tons over 12,000 miles of annual driving. Compared to an average car, each new massive SUV, like a Chevy Suburban or Ford Excursion, increases CO_2 emissions by 3.8 tons, nearly twice as much global pollution per year as avoided by an ultra-efficient small car. To really cut CO_2 emissions, higher fuel efficiency will be essential for vehicles of all sizes.

Thanks to the regulatory pressure on automakers by the U.S. Environmental Protection Agency (EPA), the California Air Resources Board (CARB), and several other state environmental agencies, cars and trucks are headed in the right direction in terms of lower smog-forming tailpipe pollution. Over the past few years, a number of companies put cleaner vehicles on the road ahead of the legal requirements. Model year 2002 continues last year's extensive nationwide sales of cars and light trucks meeting Low-Emission Vehicle (LEV) standards. Furthermore, some models such as the Toyota Camry are exclusively available at the Ultra-Low-Emission Vehicle (ULEV) standard. Most automakers are improving the emissions controls through-

Chevrolet's 3.4-liter Impala earns a spot as one of this year's Greener Choices. This LEV-certified large car has the best fuel economy in its class. *Photo: General Motors Corporation and Wieck Photo DataBase, Inc.*

out their fleets, including SUVs. Low-emission pickups and SUVs pollute more than low-emission cars, but the pollution reductions are real and will hasten the attainment of cleaner air.

Japanese automakers continue to advance the state of the art in emissions control, with super-ultra-low-emission gasoline vehicles like the Honda Accord SULEV and Nissan Sentra CA. The Toyota Prius and CVT version of the Honda Insight are also SULEVs, representing the leading edge of technology for both fuel efficiency and low pollution. Although the Prius and Insight are available in limited numbers nationwide, most SULEVs are available only in California, where gas stations are required to sell the cleaner, low-sulfur gasoline needed for advanced vehicle emissions controls to be fully effective.

Battery-powered or "plug-in" electric vehicles (EVs) earn high Green Scores, but their availability remains quite limited. EVs appeal to some consumers for their high-tech design, quiet operation, the ability to recharge at home, independence from petroleum, and simply because they are among the cleanest cars available. However, batteries have a high cost and limited range, and these constraints keep EVs from being a practical choice for most consumers.

Compressed natural gas (CNG) powered vehicles also score very well. In fact, Honda's Civic GX is this year's runner-up for greenest vehicle of the year. For buyers with access to compressed natural gas,

GREENER CHOICES 2002
A Selection of Gasoline Vehicles that Score Well

Make and Model	Specifications	Emission Standard	Fuel Economy City	Hwy	Green Score
HONDA INSIGHT	1.0L 3, auto CVT	LEV	57	56	**49**
TOYOTA PRIUS	1.5L 4, auto CVT	ULEV	52	45	**46**
HONDA CIVIC HX	1.7L 4, auto CVT	ULEV	35	40	**41**
FORD FOCUS WAGON	2.0L 4, auto	ULEV	26	32	**34**
SUZUKI ESTEEM WAGON	1.6L 4, auto	LEV	26	33	**34**
SATURN L100/200	2.2L 4, auto	ULEV	24	33	**33**
TOYOTA RAV4	2.0L 4, auto	LEV	24	29	**31**
CHEVROLET IMPALA	3.4L 6, auto	LEV	21	32	**29**
TOYOTA TACOMA	2.4L 4, auto	LEV	22	25	**28**
TOYOTA HIGHLANDER	2.4L 4, auto	LEV	22	27	**26**
CHEVROLET VENTURE*	3.4L 6, auto	LEV	19	26	**24**
FORD F-150	4.2L 6, auto	ULEV	16	20	**20**

*Also, Oldsmobile Silhouette and Pontiac Montana with same specifications.

model year 2002 offers factory-built vehicles in a variety of sizes. Although Toyota's CNG Camry is no longer being produced, the Honda Civic GX and Ford Crown Victoria are providing fleets with compact and large sedan options that achieve very low emissions levels with good driving ranges. Ford offers ULEV and even SULEV CNG options in pickups, large vans, and sport utilities, and Dodge builds natural gas-fueled trucks as well. While not having the range and cost limitations of EVs, the need for access to natural gas fueling stations means that CNG cars and trucks are usually a better choice for fleet buyers than for the average consumer.

Greener Choices for Everyone

In fact, everyone can buy green. The most environmentally friendly step you can take is really quite simple: first evaluate your needs and your budget; then look for the models with the greenest scores among the cars and trucks that meet your needs and fit your budget. Even though many of our top ratings go to electric- and natural gas-powered vehicles, every class has gasoline vehicles that score significantly better than average.

Our Greener Choices table highlights some of the top scoring gasoline vehicles in several segments of the market. It is headed up, of course, by the two hybrid cars now available, the Honda Insight and Toyota Prius. For most models, the LEV or ULEV version is the cleanest and is what we list in Greener Choices. But it is also useful to look at competing models, since within a given size class, the better vehicles often score similarly. Thus, the Greener Choices table can get you focused on the set of models that will be among the best in their class in terms of environmental friendliness.

Some models may be available with an even cleaner ULEV or SULEV rating; we've noted these in the table and they would, of course, be the best choice where they are available. Our Greener Choices list includes only automatics, even though many manual transmission versions have higher fuel economy. We've also left out econoboxes, which are, of course, very fuel efficient and economical by virtue of their small size and no-frills design. The excluded models that score even better might be good choices for some buyers. The point of the Greener Choices table is to show that there are ways to buy a cleaner and more efficient vehicle throughout the market.

Buying green does more than fulfill your own personal commitment to protect the environment. Each greener choice by an individual consumer, of course, reduces pollution directly. But the market is a give-and-take between consumers and manufacturers. As more and more consumers adopt green buying, automakers will begin to look at environmentally friendly design as an opportunity, not just an obligation. Such feedback will motivate car companies to make further investments in improved technology, so that an expanded number of green cars and trucks will be available in the years ahead.

Finally, bear in mind that the average car or light truck is likely to be operational for a dozen or more years. Even if you don't keep your new vehicle for more than a few years, your choice affects the options available for used car buyers. So instead of having yet another gas-guzzler still cruising the streets, the greener choice you make today can help cut pollution for years to come.

The Top Scorers of 2002

This year, the automatic transmission, super-ultra-low-emissions version of Honda's hybrid-electric Insight is the greenest car of the year. The natural gas-powered Honda Civic GX places second, while Toyota's battery-powered RAV4 EV scores nearly as well. The Toyota Prius hybrid stands out as the greenest gasoline-powered passenger sedan. This diverse mix of new vehicle technologies highlights the numerous avenues automakers have taken in developing greener cars and trucks. Whether they are compressed natural gas powered, hybrid gasoline-electric, plug-

GREENEST VEHICLES OF 2002

Make and Model	Specifications	Emission Standard	Fuel Economy City	Fuel Economy Hwy	Green Score
HONDA INSIGHT	1.0L 3, auto CVT[a]	SULEV	57	56	**57**
HONDA CIVIC GX	1.7L 4, auto CVT [CNG][b]	SULEV	30	34	**52**
TOYOTA RAV4 EV	Electric[c]	ZEV	3.7	2.9	**52**
TOYOTA PRIUS	1.5L 4, auto CVT	SULEV	52	45	**51**
HONDA CIVIC HX	1.7L 4, manual[d]	ULEV	36	44	**42**
TOYOTA ECHO	1.5L 4, manual[d]	LEV	34	41	**41**
NISSAN SENTRA CA	1.8L 4, auto	SULEV	27	33	**40**
HONDA CIVIC	1.7L 4, manual[d]	ULEV	33	39	**40**
MITSUBISHI MIRAGE	1.5L 4, manual	LEV	32	39	**39**
TOYOTA COROLLA	1.8L 4, manual	LEV	32	41	**39**
CHEVROLET PRIZM	1.8L 4, manual[d]	LEV	32	41	**39**
SATURN SL	1.9L 4, manual	LEV	29	40	**38**

[a] The manual transmission version of this model scores nearly as well.
[b] Compressed natural gas (CNG) vehicle fuel economy given in gasoline-equivalent miles per gallon.
[c] Electric vehicle fuel economy given in miles per kilowatt-hour.
[d] Automatic transmission versions of these models score nearly as well.

in battery-powered electric, or simply a particularly clean and efficient conventional gasoline design, it's clear that engineering with the environment in mind can be done with a host of different technologies.

Perhaps the best green consumer news is that most of this year's Greenest Vehicles list is comprised of gasoline-powered vehicles. Not long ago, the list was more populated by electric and other alternative vehicles. Among the Greenest Vehicles of model year 2002, however, are common (yet quite green) vehicles as the Chevrolet Prizm, Honda Civic, Mitsubishi Mirage, Saturn SL, Toyota Corolla, and Toyota Echo. And that's not even mentioning the two gasoline-electric hybrids, the Honda Insight and Toyota Prius, which are available nationwide and do not need any special access to electricity or another alternative fuel. Just two years ago, half of the models in the Greenest Vehicles list required an alternative fuel. This year, 10 of the 12 greenest vehicles can fill up at any gasoline station nationwide.

Electric Vehicles

Readers familiar with past editions of *ACEEE's Green Book*™ may notice that very few electric vehicles are listed this year. We only include vehicles that are both readily accessible to the public and of which a non-trivial number will actually be built in 2002. Neither progress in battery technology nor consumer demand for EVs has materialized the way that many had hoped a few years ago. In 1999, Honda discontinued its EV Plus model. A year later, GM stopped building the EV1, although the company has been re-leasing versions of the EV1 produced in previous years. Nissan's Altra EV, the Chrysler Epic electric minivan, and other models are mainly in demonstration or limited fleet use without new production runs confirmed for this year.

As this edition goes to press, the Ford Ranger EV pickup truck and Toyota RAV4 EV sport utility are the only plug-in electric vehicles with some degree of general consumer availability for the model year. Nevertheless, some car companies are about to roll out new electric minicars. Watch for announcements about special sales and leasing of vehicles such as Ford's Th!nk City, Daimler-Chrysler's Gem, and Toyota's eCom. Keep an eye on the GreenerCars.com website for preliminary Green Scores and other information about these vehicles as they are released.

Recent Electric Vehicles in *ACEEE's Green Book*™

Make and Model	Vehicle Class
GM EV1	Two Seater
Nissan Altra EV	Midsize Wagon
Chrysler Epic	Minivan
Chevy S-10 Electric	Compact Pickup
Honda EV Plus	Small SUV

The adjoining table lists some of the electric vehicles that have appeared in previous editions of this book. Some of these models may still be available for lease, especially in California. Each of these vehicles would rate at, or near, the top of their respective classes. It is mainly their cost, range, and functionality limitations that keep EVs out of the mainstream.

Some consumers raise the question, "Even though EVs have zero tailpipe emissions, they use electricity from power plants, so don't they just cause pollution somewhere else?" Yes, they do, but electric vehicles are less harmful to the environment than comparable gasoline vehicles for two main reasons.

One is that a given amount of pollution from a power plant is likely to be much less damaging to health than a similar amount from a tailpipe. To make an analogy, imagine two sidewalk cafés, one at each end of a city block. Someone is smoking a cigarette at a table at one of them. If you sit at the café at the far end of the block, you'll be less bothered by the smoke than if you are at a table in the same sidewalk café as the smoker. Similarly, pollutants from vehicle tailpipes— emitted at ground level and directly in city streets—expose people to higher concentrations of noxious fumes than do power plants, which

The Honda Insight features 21st century technology in a sporty coupe design. Its hybrid-electric drivetrain and super-ultra-low emissions make it the top scoring vehicle of the year.

Photo: American Honda Motor Co., Inc.

are generally in more remote locations and have stacks that allow the pollution to disperse before it reaches populated areas.

The other reason is that real-world emissions from gasoline vehicles are still higher than the levels set by the tailpipe standards (see "New Vehicles Aren't As Clean As You Think" on page 11). This problem is not as bad as it once was, since EPA has started requiring automakers to meet tougher tests of their cars' and light trucks' emission controls before selling them. Battery electric vehicles avoid the emissions control malfunction and degradation problems that have plagued gasoline vehicles. By comparison, emissions from electric power plants have been more reliably regulated within their permitted levels.

Nevertheless, the relative environmental advantage of electrics is being lessened by ongoing reductions in pollution from gasoline vehicles. This progress is due to both better testing and automakers' growing experience with more effective emissions control technology. In researching *ACEEE's Green Book*™, we examine the data on real-world emissions control performance. These data show that manufacturers are doing a better job of equipping their cars with controls that keep pollution low under a variety of driving conditions. The California Air Resources Board (CARB) and U.S. Environmental Protection Agency (EPA) check up on how well auto pollution controls are working in practice. Such oversight pushes the car companies to fix flaws in their vehicles' emissions control equipment. Even tighter tailpipe standards will begin taking effect in 2004. Some of the cleanest vehicles of 2002—those meeting SULEV standards—use emissions control technologies that will become commonplace over the coming years. These stringent standards, along with ongoing testing scrutiny by EPA and CARB, will further cut smog-causing pollution and save consumers money through avoided repair costs.

In contrast to smog-causing pollution, the global warming pollution from any type of vehicle depends mainly on its fuel efficiency. Carbon dioxide and other greenhouse gases are equally damaging no matter where they are emitted. An important advantage of electric vehicles is their potential for very efficient drivetrains. Electric vehicle battery capabilities remain inherently limited and costs are likely to remain relatively high. In the long run, the electric drivetrain of choice may be the fuel cell, which chemically converts a fuel directly to electricity. For now, improvements in vehicle structures and gasoline drivetrain efficiency (and when available, the extra efficiency boost of hybrid drive) provide the best choices for affordable and practical designs that cause less global warming pollution.

Light Trucks—
Most Still Score Poorly

This year, our list of the 12 Meanest Vehicles for the Environment is again dominated by large SUVs and pickups with 8-cylinder engines and 4-wheel drive. In fact, ten out of the twelve listings meet those criteria, with the two exceptions being an exotic sports car and a large van. In short, moving more metal (or moving it faster) means burning more fuel, which therefore causes more pollution unless extra steps are taken to control it. If large light trucks were used mainly for true heavy-duty hauling, fewer would be sold and their pollution would be less of a problem. But automakers have been marketing these vehicles for passenger use, pushing their sales into the millions and creating a rapidly growing source of global warming pollution.

Many automakers are now installing improved tailpipe controls on their minivans, pickups, and SUVs, which helps with part of the problem. However, dirtier versions of these light trucks, meeting the bare minimum of pollution control requirements, are still commonplace. Also, automakers are still lagging in their overall efforts to improve the fuel economy of their pickups, SUVs, and such.

MEANEST VEHICLES FOR THE ENVIRONMENT IN 2002

Make and Model	Specifications	Emission Standard	Fuel Economy City	Fuel Economy Hwy	Green Score
DODGE RAM PICKUP 2500	5.9L 8, auto 4wd	HDT	11	15	**10**
CHEVROLET SUBURBAN K2500	6.0L 8, auto 4wd	HDT	11	15	**10**
GMC YUKON XL K2500	6.0L 8, auto 4wd	HDT	12	15	**10**
CADILLAC ESCALADE /GMC YUKON DENALI [a,b]	6.0L 8, auto Awd	Tier 1	12	15	**10**
FORD EXCURSION	5.4L 8, auto 4wd	HDT-LEV	11	15	**10**
LAMBORGHINI L-147 MURCIELAGO	6.2L 12, manual 4wd [P]	Tier 1	9	13	**10**
GMC SIERRA K2500 / CHEVROLET SILVERADO K2500 [a]	6.0L 8, auto 4wd	HDT	12	15	**10**
MERCEDES-BENZ G500	5.0L 8, auto stk 4wd [P]	Tier1	12	14	**11**
DODGE RAM WAGON 2500	5.9L 8, auto	Tier 1	12	17	**11**
LEXUS LX 470 / TOYOTA LAND CRUISER [a]	4.7L 8, auto 4wd	Tier 1	13	16	**11**
CHEVROLET AVALANCHE	5.3L 8, auto 4wd	Tier 1	13	17	**12**
LINCOLN NAVIGATOR	5.4L 8, auto 4wd [P]	LEV	12	16	**12**

[P] *denotes premium gasoline.*

[a] *These vehicles are "twins"—the same base model carrying different names.*

[b] *These vehicles also tie with the Cadillac Escalade EXT and GMC Yukon XL Denali.*

Since our Green Scores reflect both tailpipe emissions and fuel economy, the high fuel consumption alone would suffice to push down the environmental ratings of the largest light trucks. Some of the largest SUVs are so massive that they are classified as heavy duty trucks (HDTs), which makes them exempt from fuel economy laws and subject to weaker tailpipe standards. The U.S. "Big 3" automakers (DaimlerChrysler, Ford, and General Motors) are increasingly taking advantage of this situation. Weight ratings of some Dodge Ram pickups and Chevrolet Suburbans have been pushed up to avoid fuel economy standards and the Ford Excursion was designed to be exempt from the standards. Led by Ford, the Big 3 have recently promised to improve the fuel economy of their light truck lines, which may help reverse this trend that has been so detrimental to the environment.

The average fuel economy of all new cars, passenger vans, SUVs, and pickups has declined over the past decade. It fell to 20.4 MPG in 2001, a level that is the lowest since 1980, and that reflects a drop of nearly 2 miles-per-gallon from the 1987–88 peak of 22.1 MPG. The main reason for this drop is that you can now buy a huge, leather-lined sport utility with any one of many luxury marquees. And while sales of such "trucks" are high, they are no more fuel efficient than their less luxurious predecessors of a decade ago.

EMISSIONS COMPARISON OF FAMILY-ORIENTED VEHICLES

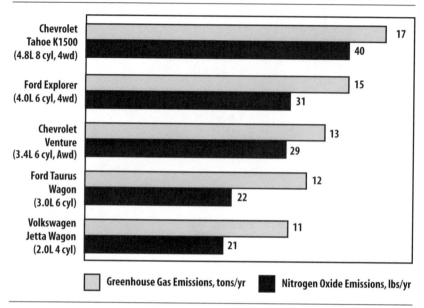

Vehicle	Greenhouse Gas Emissions, tons/yr	Nitrogen Oxide Emissions, lbs/yr
Chevrolet Tahoe K1500 (4.8L 8 cyl, 4wd)	17	40
Ford Explorer (4.0L 6 cyl, 4wd)	15	31
Chevrolet Venture (3.4L 6 cyl, Awd)	13	29
Ford Taurus Wagon (3.0L 6 cyl)	12	22
Volkswagen Jetta Wagon (2.0L 4 cyl)	11	21

All models are LEV-certified versions with automatic transmissions; pollution values are full-fuel-cycle estimates for 15,000 miles of annual driving.

If you usually carry multiple passengers in your SUV or mini-van, however, the environmental impact per passenger is lower than if you drive alone. Similarly, pickup trucks would be environmentally friendly if regularly used to carry the loads for which they are designed. Thus, a light truck can be "green" when its capacity is put to good use. For example, while large passenger vans like the Dodge Ram Wagon, Chevy Express, or GMC Savanna end up at the low end of our rankings because they score poorly, they may not really be "mean" since they're used primarily for carrying multiple passengers.

The chart above compares a range of family-oriented vehicles on the market in model year 2002. A large SUV pollutes more—and costs more—than a minivan, and it pollutes much more than a station wagon. Similar comparisons can be made among the models offered by other manufactures. Check the *Green Book* tables to find models within any size class that avoid overpowered engines and unnecessary 4-wheel drive. To buy green, think carefully about the features that you really need in a vehicle, remembering that the best choice will be the greenest vehicle that meets your needs and fits your budget.

It's a Car. It's a Truck.
It's a...Crossover Vehicle.

The last few years have seen the boundaries between cars, pickup trucks, and SUVs becoming less and less clear with the introduction of vehicles featuring both car-like handling and SUV-like spaciousness and functionality. These new so-called "crossover" vehicles, including SUVs with pickup truck beds, station wagons with SUV-like off-road abilities, and altogether new vehicles that defy most conventional categories, have been hitting the streets with great popularity. Some of these vehicles are variations on the heavy-and-rugged sort, such as Chevrolet's Avalanche, one of the latest in SUV/pickup crossbreeds. Audi's Allroad, an off-road-ready touring car, and head-turners like Saturn's VUE and Pontiac's Aztek, don't readily fit the classification of either a car or a truck. Subaru has in many ways been a segment-busting leader in crossover designs, with their Brat model in the 1980s, and more recently, their Forester and Outback models.

What this newfound popularity in crossover vehicles means for consumers is greater choice in styling and functionality. For some people, a crossover may serve as well as (or better than) a SUV or pickup truck for hauling goods around. For others, crossovers may offer the extra functionality not found in conventional cars. Either way, automakers are capitalizing on these new vehicles' uniqueness, and attempting to distinguish them from their ancestors with new names such as Sport Recreation Vehicle or Sport Activity Vehicle.

So how do crossover vehicles rank environmentally? Not surprisingly, with the exception of the massive SUV/pickup combos, they generally score better than trucks, yet worse than cars. This is in large part because fuel economies of crossovers fall between those of cars and trucks. Ultimately, the environmental benefit of crossover designs depends upon how they're used: for zipping around town, they won't be saving the planet, but they do offer a greener alternative to SUVs for ski trips to the mountains.

Because crossover vehicles don't fit exactly into the vehicle classes designated by this book, they have been listed in the class to which they are most related or that best reflects their position in the market. If you're having trouble finding a specific vehicle listing, look in the index at the back of the book. Keep in mind that while each listing's class ranking (the ✔ to ✖ symbols) compares it to others in the same vehicle class, the Green Score is not class specific, and can be used to compare vehicles among any class. So the Green Score will often be the best way to evaluate crossover models. For example, the LEV-certified, automatic version of Chrysler's PT Cruiser has a Green Score of 26, which ranks below the average-scoring small wagons such as Volvo's V40 that scores 29. Nevertheless, the PT Cruiser is greener than a compact SUV like Hyundai's Santa Fe, which has a Green Score of 25 in its automatic configuration.

What About Diesels?

It is still an open question whether diesel engines can be made clean enough to extensively exploit their efficiency advantage in the U.S. market. Today's diesels, such as Volkswagen's New Beetle GLS TDi (turbocharged direct-injection), score "Inferior" in *Green Book* ratings even though they are more fuel-efficient than their gasoline counterparts. The New Beetle 1.9-liter TDi diesel automatic rates 34 MPG in the city and 44 MPG on the highway, for an overall average of 38 MPG. That's 50 percent better than the 25 MPG average for the New Beetle with a 2.0-liter gasoline engine. But EPA allows the diesel version to emit five times as much nitrogen oxide (NO_x) pollution as the gasoline-powered New Beetle, which now qualifies as both a low-emission vehicle (LEV) and ultra-low-emission vehicle (ULEV) nationwide.

Automakers are working to clean up the diesel vehicle. For example, Ford is developing a version of the Focus sedan that uses advanced control technologies targeted to meet California's upcoming ULEV II standards. They have equipped their laboratory test car with a special NO_x clean-up device in which a solution of urea in water is sprayed on the catalyst to selectively reduce NO_x from the exhaust stream. The vehicle also has a catalytic, soot-trapping filter to remove fine particles. Widespread use of such systems is still some years away, particularly if a new chemical such as urea needs to be widely distributed along with ultra-clean diesel fuel. Engineers at Ford and other companies trying to slash diesel emissions are making up for lost time, since today's gasoline engines benefit from over three decades of experience with ever-tighter pollution standards.

Bi- and Flex-Fuel Vehicles

A number of automakers are now offering vehicles with bi-fuel capability, meaning the ability to run on either an alternative fuel or gasoline. For example, some pickup trucks can be set to run on compressed natural gas (CNG) or gasoline, depending on what fuel is available to the driver. Flexible-fuel vehicles (FFVs) can automatically detect the fuel put into the tank, typically an alcohol-gasoline blend such as E85 or M85 (85 percent ethanol or methanol, respectively, with 15 percent gasoline).

ACEEE's Green Book™ does not provide listings for bi- and flex-fuel vehicles since their environmental performance is not generally different than that of their gasoline-only counterparts. In terms of tailpipe emissions, a bi-fuel CNG vehicle may be cleaner when running on CNG than when running on gasoline. Some FFVs may be cleaner when running on their alternative fuel, but in practice this rarely happens. Some automakers are making FFVs widely available to the general market in a number of models. But since alternative fuels (such as E85) are available in very few locations—many FFV drivers do not even know of their vehicle's alternative fuel capability—FFVs are operated almost exclusively with gasoline. Nevertheless, automakers are getting higher credits toward their fuel economy requirements with every FFV they sell. Ironically, such sales are causing more pollution overall because of the corresponding decrease in fleetwide fuel economy. Thus, the availability of FFVs, while perhaps well intentioned, is resulting in higher nationwide gasoline consumption, higher oil dependence, and worse global warming pollution than would otherwise occur.

Green by Design

Whathat makes one car greener than another? High fuel economy is one factor. A vehicle that meets the strictest tailpipe standards is greener than one meeting weaker standards. Being built in a clean factory with safe, non-toxic substances and using a high fraction of recycled materials are further factors for environmental friendliness. The key to progress on all of these fronts is design with the environment in mind. Sophisticated engine controls and advanced transmissions; streamlined body styles and strong, lightweight materials; and hybrid-electric drive—a bounty of technologies are available to help make cars and trucks "Green by Design."

Design improvements developed by automotive engineers are the main reason that cars have improved so much over the past generation. Thirty years ago, the average new car got no more than 13 miles per gallon. Its pollution controls were crude and unreliable. Indeed, vehicles in general were hardly reliable by today's standards. Cars were heavier but far less safe. Comfort and convenience features now standard in common models were absent from all but the most expensive luxury mobiles.

This year, the U.S. automobile fleet, even though it is now half "trucks," goes 50 percent farther per gallon of gasoline than in 1970, with one-tenth or less the amount of tailpipe pollution. Most auto factories are cleaner, too; less energy is consumed in making the materials and running the factories. At least in the United States, under the watchful eyes of unions, environmentalists, and the EPA, autoworkers and their communities are exposed to fewer toxic chemicals than were their parents and grandparents. Three-quarters of automotive steel gets recycled. New plastics and composites are being designed with recycling in mind, and recycled plastics are showing up in new parts such as bumpers.

All of these improvements are due to better design. Engines are more efficient, with better components, electronic controls, and fuel injection instead of carburetors. Catalytic converters—helped by lead-free gasoline and working hand-in-hand with newer engines—filter out most of the worst pollution. Chassis and body parts are stronger and lighter, providing smoother, quieter rides, superior handling, and better crashworthiness. Radial tires grip and handle better while cutting down rolling resistance. Streamlined bodies save gas and help cut pollution at highway speeds while reducing wind noise. Many of the cars and trucks that score well in our green ratings do so because of one or more aspects of improved technology.

While the *Green Book* helps you find the best vehicles of today, it also makes it clear that cars and trucks still have some distance to go in terms of environmental friendliness. This need to improve is particularly true when it comes to fuel consumption and global warming. The fuel economy of cars and light trucks did increase from 1973 through the mid-1980s. But since then, it has been slowly declining as automakers have put most of their technology improvements into higher performance and other amenities. New vehicles produce less pollution per mile than those of years gone by, but the amount of driving continues to grow. Just as we expect ever more comfort, performance, and reliability, it's reasonable to expect new cars and trucks to do an ever better job on environmental quality. A look at some of the greener model year 2002 vehicles illustrates technologies that represent the best engineering of today and point the way toward greener designs tomorrow.

Greener Tech Today

Automakers revamp their vehicles every several years. They also introduce all-new, ground-up models. Such new designs and redesigns represent the cutting edge of automotive engineering. A look under the skin of recent models reveals an array of refinements. Many either improve efficiency or maintain it in the face of added power, size, and luxury. Step back from a revamped model and you'll see that it is more aerodynamic than the model it replaced. Under the hood, the new engine is likely to be more efficient and cleaner, as well as quieter and more powerful, than before. Chances are that an advanced transmission is helping the engine burn less fuel per mile with smoother, electronically controlled shifting.

Some of the most important refinements are often the most hidden. Many different materials go into making today's cars and trucks. Steel is still the foundation of most vehicles. But steel and steel structures have come a long way over the past generation. For example, High-Strength Lightweight Alloy (HSLA) steels enable engineers to tailor the strength, flexibility, corrosion resistance, ease of shaping and joining, and other properties of parts to get the most performance out of the least mass. Expanded use of these higher grades of steel, as well as innovative forming and welding techniques, enable car makers to build bodies that weigh less, are more crashworthy, more rigid, and

More and more engine blocks are being cast from aluminum, such as the Toyota Highlander's shown here. The result is a ripple effect of weight savings that help improve efficiency and reduce emissions.

Photo: Toyota Motor Sales, U.S.A.

less prone to noise, vibration, or a harsh ride. Steel is also extensively recycled, reducing pollution due to the production of new materials.

For a number of components, iron and steel are being replaced with lighter metals such as aluminum, magnesium, and titanium. Engine blocks are a good example where aluminum has been steadily replacing iron. A heavy engine does no good. It's just more mass to haul around; it places an added burden on the rest of a vehicle's front end rather than contributing to structural strength and safety. Getting more power out of each pound of engine is one of the best examples of "hidden" green design.

From advanced plastics that cut both weight and cost to sophisticated electronics, many other design tricks can be best summed up as simply nifty engineering. Automakers are also using better catalytic converters and smart engine controls to progressively trim tailpipe pollution, resulting in greater availability of various Low-Emission Vehicles (LEVs).

The "best of the best" are, of course, hybrid-electric vehicles. Two are on the market in model year 2002. The Toyota Prius is the world's first mass-produced hybrid-electric car and sets a record as the most fuel-efficient compact sedan. The Honda Insight was the first hybrid to reach U.S. shores and this sporty two-seater reigns as the overall fuel economy champion. Honda will be introducing a hybrid-electric version of the Civic in spring 2002 as an early model year 2003 car. Later in this chapter we'll preview the Civic hybrid and other hybrids heading into showrooms over the next few years. We'll also gaze through an engineering crystal ball at fuel cell vehicles and other futuristic options.

Earth-Friendlier Family Sedans

The midsize sedan is in many ways the heart of the car market. Used by families, singles, and many businesses as well, this tried-and-true body style provides excellent value, respectable efficiency (especially when compared to trendy light trucks), good safety, and ever-better performance and amenities.

Competition in the midsize segment means that differences among cars can be subtle. Most vehicles provide similar space and functionality. Comfortable seating for five and ample trunk space plus just-fine everyday pep and handling are assumed for any midsize car. Option packages add more convenience, "automatic everything," and yet faster performance. But unless you're splitting seconds with a stopwatch, you might never notice many of the performance differences. If you are one of those who hold onto their cars for 10 years or so, the performance differences are marked. Comparing a 2002 car with a similar model from, say, model year 1992, you're likely to find that a second and a half has been shaved from the 0–60 mph time, with average midsize cars now beating the 10-second mark.

The close competition in the midsize segment also means that differences in environmental friendliness are subtle. As throughout the market, consumers are presented with a trade-off in terms of power performance versus fuel economy, and fuel economy is a crucial component of green design.

The Fuel-Efficient Engine Advantage

Most of our "Best of 2002" family sedans have 4-cylinder engines, so they are not the fastest on the lot. But put in perspective, they provide plenty of zip without needing to show-off in a horsepower war. Take the Toyota Camry with its 2.4-liter engine—this twin-cam inline four puts out 157 hp and delivers up to 162 foot-pounds of torque. Its nationwide ULEV availability helps put this edition of the Camry in our "Best of 2002" list. Unfortunately, Toyota did not improve the Camry's fuel economy, which remains at 23 MPG city and 32 MPG highway, even though the new model is larger and peppier than last year's.

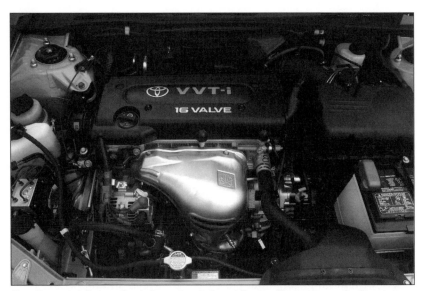

The all-new 2.4-liter engine in Toyota's redesigned Camry offers an array of refinements over its predecessor without a sacrifice in fuel economy or emissions level.

Photo: Toyota Motor Sales, U.S.A.

One reason for the good performance is that this new power plant features a host of refinements, including Toyota's "Variable Valve Timing with intelligence" (VVT-i). This engine is a far cry from traditional four-cylinder expectations. Notably smooth-running, it delivers 21 horsepower more than the previous four-cylinder Camry engine. Displacement is up, with a nine percent increase over the 2.2 liters of last year's model, but power is up even more, a 15 percent boost. Torque increases roughly in proportion to displacement, but Toyota's VVT-i delivers the peak torque at 4,000 RPM rather than 4,400, enhancing both smoothness and efficiency. With the new Camry being more spacious, the new engine pushes more car faster than the 2001 model without a trade-off in fuel economy.

In spite of the engine's higher power and the addition of variable valve control, the Camry's new 2.4-liter engine weighs under 250 pounds, over 50 pounds less than the previous engine. This hidden efficiency gain is made possible by advanced aluminum die-casting techniques. The engine is cast in two pieces. Fittings for the power steering pump and air conditioner are built into the block, avoiding the need for mounting brackets as a way to cut engine noise and vibration as well as mass.

Another hidden engine efficiency gain comes from an offset crank shaft. This trick is also used in Toyota's Prius and Echo engines. By setting the crankshaft off to the side (by just under half an inch, in this case) rather than directly beneath the cylinder bore line, friction due to the piston pressing more against one side of the cylinder wall is reduced. And any extra bit of energy that doesn't get wasted in friction goes into getting more engine output. The result is an engine that is technically more efficient, but also represents a lost opportunity for greater greenness in that Toyota put all of its efforts into more power instead of more miles per gallon.

Improved Body and Interior

The Camry has been the best-selling car in America, from 1997–2000, but the Honda Accord and Ford Taurus—each of which has also held the crown in recent years—are hot on its heels. So in redesigning the Camry, Toyota targeted improvements in several areas. Designers wanted a larger interior that was also quieter and more comfortable than before, riding on a body and chassis that excels in ride and handling, dynamic performance, acceleration and braking, and steering feel. Toyota sought to maintain the ultra-low (ULEV) emissions ratings it introduced on all Camrys last year and also stay among the top midsize offerings in fuel economy, but these green metrics were not targeted for improvement. Thus, the design challenge was to deliver the other enhancements without decreasing fuel economy or increasing emissions

So, in addition to a new engine, Toyota developed a brand-new platform, the Camry's first "ground-up" redesign in 10 years. The body is wider and taller, with a wheelbase that is two inches longer, providing a more spacious interior. The new design also raises the "hip-point," the distance from the ground that the seat situates a driver's hip joint—this change makes it easier to get in and out of the car. To help maintain fuel efficiency while upsizing, Toyota used refined materials and design techniques to minimize weight increase. The engineers also cut the Camry's drag coefficient, from 0.30 down to 0.284; the drag coefficient measures a vehicle's "slipperiness" when moving through the air and is important for fuel economy at highway speeds.

Edging Toward Eco-Improved SUVs

By some reckonings, the sport utility vehicle is the ecological "bad boy" of today's society. Many have noted the irony of how a lifestyle vehicle linked to a love of nature and the great outdoors has been such a cause of environmental backwardness in the car and truck market. Our Green Scores bear this out: 7 of the 12 Meanest Vehicles for the Environment this year are SUVs. But clearly, the SUV

Sleek redesign of the 2002 Camry lowered its drag coefficient—a measurement of the vehicle's "slipperiness" in the air—from 0.30 to 0.284, improving its fuel economy at highway speeds.   *Photo: Toyota Motor Sales, U.S.A.*

taps a deep well of consumer aspirations. The *Green Book* ratings can help sort out the choices so that—to stretch the analogy—we need not tap quite so many oil wells in the process.

As in most segments, SUVs compete closely with each other on multiple factors, but greenness isn't one of them. The differences in fuel economy among SUVs of similar size, function, and price are rarely large. Nevertheless, the segment is growing more diverse with the emergence of sport wagons and other "crossover" styles that offer higher efficiency with equivalent functionality to older models.

Building a Better Box on Wheels

The middle of the sport utility market, and the most crowded segment, is the midsize SUV. This year, the Toyota Highlander and two General Motors siblings, the Pontiac Aztek and Buick Rendezvous, make the upper reaches of our Best of 2002 list for midsize SUVs. A key feature of these newer designs is their unitized body. Such "unibody" construction integrates a rigid body structure with an underbody that serves as a frame to which chassis and suspension components are attached.

The earliest vehicles to define the SUV segment, such as the original Jeep Cherokee, Ford Explorer, and Chevy Blazer—as well as ancestors like the Toyota Land Cruiser or the Land Rover—were built by placing a separate body on top of a truck frame. This "body-on-frame"

43

Pontiac's Aztek is a top-rated midsize SUV in terms of Green Score that also earns top billing among SUVs for rollover safety. *Photo: General Motors Corporation and Wieck Photo DataBase, Inc.*

construction was also the way most cars were built, until unibody construction swept the car market in the 1980s. The Jeep Grand Cherokee was the first mainstream, midsize U.S. SUV to adopt unibody structure when it was introduced in 1992. Compared to body-on-frame design, the unibody approach improves both efficiency and safety. A given size unibody can be built with less steel and can be better optimized for crashworthiness than an equivalent body-on-frame.

Introduced last year, the Pontiac Aztek is an example of a unibody SUV that takes structural design a further step forward. Along with its platform partner, the newly-introduced Buick Rendezvous, the Aztek is among our top-scoring midsize SUVs. It illustrates how many seemingly modest refinements can add up to a design that is quite fuel-efficient for its size. Pontiac emphasizes the versatility and functionality of the Aztek's design, and fitting generous interior space inside a box of given exterior dimensions is part of that functionality. It's accomplished by what car designers call good "packaging." That means ways to fit you, your family, your friends, and your stuff comfortably inside the vehicle. Efficient packaging contributes to green design because it provides a more useful space in a structure of a given size, using less material, and so less mass, while maintaining comfort and safety.

The Aztek has a wide and flat load floor, positioned relatively low to the road for ease of loading and unloading. A bonus of the lower, wider design is greater stability on the road. The 4-wheel drive Aztek earns four stars in the National Highway Traffic Safety Administra-

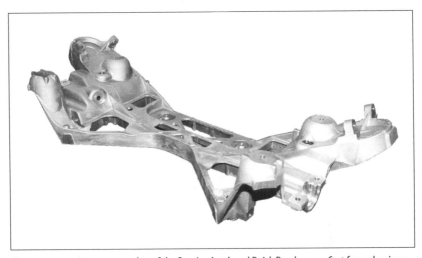

The rear suspension cross member of the Pontiac Aztek and Buick Rendezvous. Cast from aluminum alloy, this award-winning part saves weight while improving suspension performance.

Photo: American Foundry Society

tion's rollover ratings, making it the best-ranked SUV to date. It has built-in storage areas as well as modular seating that can be readily repositioned for different uses. These seating systems show how components designed to make life easier for the owner can offer a bonus for the environment. Flipping and folding the seats, or taking them out for extra cargo space, is a lot easier if they are lighter. And of course, lighter means leaner in terms of fuel use.

Mass-Saving Magic

If you were to look under the rear of the Aztek or Rendezvous, you'll find a key part of the suspension called a cross member. This complex part runs between the rear wheels and has numerous cutouts and mounting points for shock absorbers and other suspension components. Cross members have been traditionally made by welding together stamped steel pieces. Many mountings required separate brackets, involving not only many sub-parts but also extra assembly steps. The cross member used on the Aztek represents the kind of advances in materials and manufacturing processes that can yield major, simultaneous improvements in performance, weight saving, and assembly cost savings that get passed on as benefits for the car buyer.

This part, developed by Hayes Lemmerz International, Inc. in collaboration with GM, won one of last year's American Foundry Society awards for ingenuity and quality. It is cast as a single piece using an aluminum alloy in a permanent mold that builds the mountings for many suspension components right into the cross member. The precision casting process provides better quality in terms of strength, part dimensions, and integrity, while helping to improve the vehicle's ride and handling. It also saves weight compared to a multi-part steel cross member assembly. Although pound-for-pound aluminum costs more than steel, the added functionality and reduced assembly work made possible with the casting ends up saving cost overall.

And talk about really hidden design features: do you ever worry about what's in the floor of your vehicle? Between the carpet on which you put your feet and a vehicle's underbody is padding known as the floor carpet underlay. It is important for damping out road noise and body vibrations, and is also important for the look, feel, and durability of a vehicle's floor. The Pontiac Aztek and Buick Rendezvous feature a floor carpet underlay that is manufactured using a new, continuous cutting process. This technology, developed by GM's supplier Foamex International, makes it possible for an entire floor carpet underlay to be cost-effectively fabricated as a single, lightweight polyurethane foam component, contoured to perfectly fit the shape of the floor pan. This process also saves weight—nearly 10 pounds in the Aztek—illustrating yet another innovation that contributes to greener design.

CVT Meets SUV

Transmissions are another technology that is all too easy to take for granted. Modern transmissions last much longer than older ones and under normal use are not something most new car shoppers need to worry about. What does matter are smooth shifting, good performance, and fuel economy. Manual transmissions traditionally provide better mileage than automatics. But that's beginning to change with a new generation of electronically controlled automatics that can use their smarts to operate a car or truck engine at higher efficiency.

A big job of any transmission is striking the right balance between responsiveness and efficiency by matching a vehicle's driving speed to the engine speed. Different gears cover different gear ranges, and getting from one gear to another is where smarts come into play. Having more gears provides a better match and less abrupt shifts. That's why the number of speeds in transmissions has been increasing. Three-speeds are nearly all gone. For automatics, many newer designs now have five speeds, and leading-edge models have six.

But some transmissions take the leap to an "infinite" number of speeds. This feat is accomplished in what is called a *continuously*

The Saturn VUE's "VTi" transmission marks the first use of a continuously variable transmission (CVT) in the SUV market. *Photo: General Motors Corporation and Wieck Photo DataBase, Inc.*

variable transmission, or CVT. The most common kind of CVT uses steel belts on pulleys that can change their diameter to allow for a smoothly changing range of gear ratios. A few have been on the market in compact cars, where the CVT's past torque limitations could be accommodated. For example, a CVT is part of what places the Honda Civic HX as one of the most fuel-efficient among compact coupes. Honda uses a CVT for the automatic version of the Insight, which reigns as the top-scoring gasoline vehicle overall.

This year, continuously variable transmission technology takes a step forward by appearing in 2.2-liter 4-cylinder versions of Saturn's new VUE sport utility vehicle. GM designates this CVT the "VTi" option on the VUE, and the company notes that it is slated for high-volume production and extensive use in several markets globally. With a transmission like the VTi, stepping on the gas produces added power without any noticeable jolt from downshifting. A CVT also has a much greater range between its lowest and highest ratios than a conventional automatic, which is one reason why it helps raise fuel economy.

Although a conventional automatic isn't offered on the 2.2-liter Saturn VUE for direct comparison, GM notes that the VTi transmission provides 7 percent better fuel economy than if a 4-speed automatic were used. As a result, the Saturn VUE VTi matches the 5-speed manual version of the vehicle in fuel economy. An added boon for a CVT is that it facilitates tight tailpipe pollution control. While the manual version of the VUE achieves an LEV emissions rating, the VTi versions meet the tighter ULEV standards nationwide. Although the Saturn VUE is billed as a compact SUV (and priced accordingly and affordably), it fits at the bigger end of that segment's size range. Thus, it can make for a greener choice if you are looking for something larger than a traditional "cute ute" and want the added space without the fuel cost and price tag of many midsize SUVs.

Hybrids are Happening

Hybrid-electric vehicles combine an electric motor with an internal combustion engine. The result is an extra-efficient, no-compromises powertrain that takes advantage of the efficiency benefits of electric drive as well as the performance of a gasoline engine.

Model year 2002 sees two of these advanced technology vehicles offered in the market. The Honda Insight, a two-seater coupe featuring Honda's Integrated Motor Assist (IMA) hybrid system, is the greenest car now available. The Toyota Prius, introduced here last summer after three years in the Japanese market, is the greenest family sedan and uses the Toyota Hybrid System (THS). More hybrid-electric vehicles are on the near horizon. Next up will be an IMA hybrid version of the Honda Civic. Other announcements include SUVs and pickups from the Big 3 promised by 2003–2004. The way this technology is advancing, we might well see some additional HEV entries over the next few years.

Toyota Prius

The world's first mass-produced hybrid electric vehicle is a product of many technological and design advances. But it is its powertrain, which combines an efficient gasoline engine with a smooth and quiet electric motor, that gives the Prius its biggest boost in green performance.

The heart of the Prius powertrain is contained in what is in effect the car's automatic transmission. This "Toyota Hybrid System" (THS) device is no ordinary transmission. Inside is a special "planetary" gear set coupled to an electric motor and a generator, all operated under computer control. The sophisticated combination of electrical and mechanical components makes it, in effect, a super-smart transmission. But it is really more than a transmission, since it also sends power back and forth among the engine, wheels, motor, generator, and battery.

HYBRID ELECTRIC VEHICLES

HERE TODAY

Make and Model	Class	Specifications	Emissions	Avg. Fuel Economy	Green Score
Toyota Prius	Compact Sedan	1.5L 4, auto CVT	SULEV	48	**51**
Honda Insight	Two Seater	1.0L 3, auto CVT[1]	SULEV	56	**57**

ON THE WAY

Make and Model	Class	Specifications	Emissions	Fuel Economy[2]	Expected
Honda Civic Hybrid	Compact Sedan	1.3L 4, auto CVT	ULEV	50	2002
Ford Escape HEV	Compact SUV	2.0L 4, auto	SULEV	35	2003
Dodge Durango HEV	Midsize SUV	3.9L 6, auto	—	17	2003
Dodge Contractor Special	Fullsize Pickup	5.2L 8, auto	—	18	2004
GM "Epsilon" SUV	Midsize SUV	3.6L 6, auto	—	30	2004
GM Silverado/Sierra	Fullsize Pickup	5.3L 8, auto	—	18	2004

[1] Also available in 5-speed manual version with improved fuel economy—see tables.
[2] These fuel economy estimates are approximate, given as average of city and highway label values.

When starting from a stop, the Prius's gasoline engine need not come on at all; the battery supplies power to the electric drive motor. The engine also stops when the car is idling, coasting, or at other times when low power is needed. This "idle off" feature of the hybrid system results in a 13 percent fuel savings in city driving. The engine restarts quickly and quietly whenever more power is needed. The gasoline engine also runs as needed to keep the battery charged.

Among the benefits of hybrid drive is regenerative braking, which converts wheel rotation into electricity. When the car is coasting down or when the brakes are applied, the electric motor acts as a generator, recapturing energy. The recovered energy is stored in the battery rather than lost as friction in the brakes. During the stop-and-go of city driving, this feature provides up to a 19 percent improvement in fuel efficiency.

The Prius gasoline engine itself is of a special design, achieving very high efficiency for its displacement while also trimming weight. The 1.5-liter four-cylinder engine produces 70 horsepower at 4500 RPM. Limiting the engine to this relatively low-RPM redline enables the use of lighter components and reduces friction. Toyota could take this approach because they didn't have to maximize the engine's power, since the electric motor provides over 40 horsepower of additional muscle. A crankshaft offset from the cylinder

49

The Prius powertrain packs a high-efficiency engine together with the Toyota Hybrid System— containing a motor, generator, and planetary gear set—into a similar amount of space as a conventional engine and transmission.   *Photo: Toyota Motor Sales, U.S.A.*

centerline is another friction-cutting feature, one that is also used on Toyota's new Camry and Echo inline fours. Finally, a sophisticated emissions control system and advanced catalyst cut tailpipe pollution to Super-Ultra-Low-Emission (SULEV) levels. Thus, the Prius is both far cleaner at the tailpipe as well as much more efficient than average in fuel use.

Honda Hybrids:
Insight First, Civic on the Way

The Honda Insight is the most fuel-efficient gasoline vehicle you can buy, even among small cars. It is also a technological showcase, featuring not only hybrid drive but also advances in every other key vehicle system. To engineer the Insight for record fuel economy, Honda focused on three broad areas of design.

First, a strong, lightweight aluminum structure and highly streamlined body reduce the overall power needed for moving the car, accounting for a 30 percent efficiency increase. The lower power requirements that go with lower weight permit a smaller and less costly powertrain for a given level of performance.

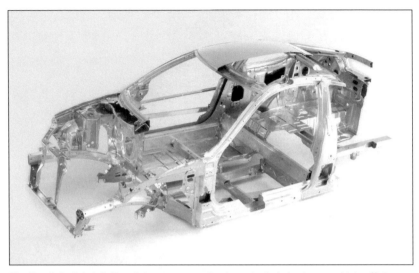

The Honda Insight's lightweight yet strong aluminum body helps boost vehicle efficiency while providing superior crashworthiness. Advanced aluminum structures hold great promise as a way to build safe and durable lightweight frames for vehicles of all sizes.

Photo: American Honda Motor Co., Inc. and PR Newswire

Second, the Insight's 1.0-liter VTEC-E gasoline engine is highly efficient by virtue of its compact size and the use of variable valve control, lean combustion, and advanced techniques for cutting friction. The engine enhancements provide another 30 percent efficiency increase.

Third, the Insight's electric drive components—motor, battery, and controls—recover braking energy and boost power, so that good performance is achieved with the smaller engine. The hybrid drivetrain also allows the engine to stop when it is idling and full power is not needed. These features provide the remaining 25 percent step up to the 85 percent total efficiency increase demonstrated by the Insight's design.

The Honda Insight's lightweight structural innovations represent an important facet of the automotive future. Various combinations of materials are being investigated for cutting vehicle weight while enhancing safety and structural performance. One of the best options is optimized use of aluminum. The front and rear sections of the Insight's frame use advances, such as hexagonal sections adapted from race car frames, to absorb crash energy. These techniques exploit aluminum's special properties, enabling a controlled cushioning that protects occupants from crash forces. The inner structure has pillars and beams to form a rigid cage around the driver and passenger, resisting intrusion and deformation. As a result, even though it is a small car, the Honda Insight earns 4-star ratings for both frontal and side-impact crashworthiness.

Building on their experience with the Insight, Honda engineers will couple a 1.3-liter lean-burn gasoline engine to an improved electric motor for the model year 2003 Civic hybrid. Fuel economy is expected to reach 50 miles per gallon.

Photo: American Honda Motor Co., Inc.

The Insight's gasoline engine—a 1.0-liter, 3-cylinder, 12-valve design—is one of the most efficient gasoline engines in production. It puts out 67 horsepower, nearly 20 percent more per liter than the average new car and light truck, all the more remarkable because it is tuned for high efficiency. In the automatic version of the Insight, a continuously variable transmission (CVT) provides for smooth, responsive, and efficient coupling of the gasoline engine and hybrid drive to drive the front wheels.

The heart of the hybrid in Honda's case is called "Integrated Motor Assist" (IMA) because an electric motor is merged right onto the back of the engine, assisting it with up to 30 foot-pounds of added torque. Power assist is one of the key fuel-saving techniques of hybrid drive. Energy is saved if one uses a small engine (like the 1.0-liter Insight engine); it is also saved if an engine is operated as much as possible at low RPM. But a smaller engine has less torque, and high RPM provides high power. Thus, using the efficient electric motor to put back the torque, especially at low RPM, provides the performance that would otherwise be lost. The IMA system also recaptures braking energy and allows the engine to be turned off when the car is stopped but restart quickly as soon as power is needed.

This edition of the *Green Book* goes to press just before final specs on the upcoming Honda Civic hybrid are to be announced. While the Civic hybrid will be designated model year 2003, the first cars are slated to hit showrooms this spring. To develop a hybrid-electric Civic, Honda made numerous advances, building on the experience gained with the Insight. The Civic hybrid will also feature the first U.S. application of a lean-burn dual spark-ignition gasoline engine. Called iDSI by Honda, it represents yet another advance in the state-of-the-art for engine efficiency.

The IMA system to be installed on the Civic is an improved version with even better technical efficiency than the first-generation IMA system used on the Honda Insight. A basic function of the IMA is to provide extra torque during acceleration and other times of heavy engine load. The motor assist shuts down at cruising speeds when engine load is lower.

Like all hybrid drives, the IMA provides regenerative braking, so the motor acts as a generator to convert captured energy into electricity. But an innovation on the iDSI engine enables the valves to disengage and seal off up to three cylinders during deceleration. This cylinder-idling feature reduces the friction inside the engine that otherwise slows a car when you lift your foot off the accelerator. Since such engine braking represents lost energy, this feature allows more energy to be regenerated through electric braking. As in the Insight, the Civic's engine-IMA system also uses idle stop. The engine shuts off automatically if the vehicle comes to a complete halt and then restarts immediately when the accelerator pedal is pressed.

Honda made many other refinements for the new Civic IMA system, yielding better efficiency, more compact components, and lower cost. Improvements to the internal magnetic coils of the ultra-thin DC brushless motor, which boasts the world's highest output density and overall efficiency, achieve 30 percent greater torque than the version used in the Insight. The power electronics have been redesigned, cutting their weight by 30 percent and cutting volume by 40 percent. The efficiency of the battery modules has been increased and the battery's peripheral systems have been made more compact as well.

Putting it all together, the Honda Civic hybrid will use its 1.3-liter iDSI engine with a CVT and the IMA system to yield a projected 50 MPG while meeting the California ULEV standard. Watch *ACEEE's Green Book*™ online at GreenerCars.com for updates on the

Civic hybrid, including its preliminary Green Score once it is on the market.

Ford Escape HEV

The Ford Motor Company is planning to introduce a hybrid-electric version of its Escape SUV in 2003. The Escape HEV will feature an electric drivetrain combined with a new version of Ford's four-cylinder "Zetec" gasoline engine tuned to run at extra-high efficiency. Combining this engine with a 87 hp electric motor will enable the Escape HEV to perform just as well as a V-6 version while achieving 35–40 MPG in city driving and up to 30 MPG on the highway. Today's comparable Ford Escape V-6 is rated at 19 MPG city and 24 MPG highway.

Ford's design strategy for the Escape uses the electric drive to supplement the power of the gasoline engine, enabling the engine to be designed for higher efficiency than it could when used without a hybrid powertrain. The Escape HEV will use a special version of Ford's Zetec inline four-cylinder engine. Existing versions of this engine are used in the 4-cylinder versions of today's Escape as well as the Ford Focus. The Zetec has a lightweight, low-friction design that can achieve significant gains in fuel economy without compromising on responsiveness and drivability. Different version of the engine are used for different purposes. For example, Ford's "Special Vehicle Team" (SVT) version of the Focus uses a suped-up 2.0-liter Zetec engine that puts out 170 hp. By comparison, the engines used in the Focus ZX3 and Escape XLS models put out just under 130 hp.

An opposite tack is taken for the version of the Zetec being developed for the hybrid Escape. Because up to 87 hp of extra power can be provided by the electric motor, the engine is designed to use a special "Atkinson" cycle that is significantly more efficient than a conventional four-stroke gasoline engine cycle. This type of engine design sacrifices torque—but torque is the strong suit of an electric motor. As a result, the Escape's hybrid drive system puts back the power and responsiveness that would otherwise be sacrificed with the special engine cycle. A similar approach is used in the Toyota Prius, which also has an Atkinson cycle engine.

In addition to the 87 hp (65 kW) electric drive motor, the Ford Escape's hybrid system will have a 28 kW generator, providing regenerative braking and battery charging from the engine. A special 300-volt battery, to be supplied by Sanyo, will be packaged under the rear floor of the Escape HEV, without any loss of cargo space. The hybrid system will also be able to drive the vehicle at low speeds as well as turn off the combustion engine when the vehicle is stopped while instantly restarting it as soon as motive power is needed. In terms of tailpipe pollution, the Escape HEV is being designed to qualify as a Super-Ultra-Low-Emission Vehicle (SULEV) under California standards.

General Motors Hybrid Pickup and SUV

GM has promised a hybrid system as an option on its Chevy Silverado and GMC Sierra pickups in 2004. The result will be a fully capable, V-8-powered pickup truck that hauls just as much as its conventional gasoline-only counterparts, offers supplemental power outlets, and gets better fuel economy. The truck will use GM's 5.3-liter "Vortec" V-8, one of the larger engines in the Silverado and Sierra 1500-series. Its hybrid design is not used to downsize or de-rate the engine for extra-high efficiency. Instead, a modest efficiency improvement is obtained from this hybrid design, which integrates the electric motor/generator between the engine and transmission. The system doubles as the starter and allows the engine to be turned off during idle; it also recaptures energy of motion when the brakes are applied.

Model year 2002 Silverados with the 5.3-liter engine have a city-plus-highway average fuel economy of 15 MPG with 4-wheel drive and 16 MPG with 2-wheel drive. GM's hybrid versions will have up to 15 percent better fuel economy, suggesting averages of 17–18 MPG. That's even higher than today's version of the trucks with the smaller, 4.3-liter base engines, which average about 7 percent more fuel efficient than their 5.3-liter counterparts.

The Silverado and Sierra hybrid pickups will use a 42-volt system, with the integrated starter/generator charging an advanced lead-acid battery pack. Solid-state electronics control not only the charging and engine restart functions, but also boost the current to 110 volts at up to 20 amps for the supplemental power outlets. The plugs can be used for power tools, camping equipment, or other recreational gear.

GM will offer an even more sophisticated hybrid system in a new SUV slated to debut in 2004. The vehicle is being designed as one version of a mid-sized platform code-named Epsilon. This version of GM's hybrid system is called "ParadiGM" and it may eventually be used in a variety of vehicles, including SUVs, new crossover vehicles, and traditional sedans.

The new SUV will use a ParadiGM configuration that couples a 3.6-liter V-6 gasoline engine with a hybrid drive package containing a pair of electric motors connected to a battery pack. The V-6 engine will put out 220 hp, with a boost of up to 32 hp more coming from the electric motors. GM projects that the new hybrid SUV will deliver about 20 percent better fuel economy than a non-hybrid version of this vehicle. The result will be roughly 30 MPG as an average of the city and highway MPG label ratings, but most of the efficiency gain will come in city driving. But the design may also push boundaries on hot performance, since GM expects an SUV powered by the ParadiGM powertrain to accelerate from 0–60 mph in just over 7 seconds.

DaimlerChrysler Hybrids

DaimlerChrysler's first announced hybrid vehicle for the U.S. market will be a HEV version of the Durango SUV. The vehicle will combine an 89 hp electric motor with a 175 hp, 3.9-liter V-6 gasoline engine. Thus, its performance will match that of a Durango equipped with DaimlerChrysler's 5.9-liter V-8, while its fuel economy will be 20 percent higher. The result will be 17 MPG in average city plus highway driving, compared to an average of 14 MPG with today's 4-wheel drive V-8 Durango.

Slated for introduction in 2003, the Durango hybrid SUV will accomplish its efficiency gain by using a unique, split hybrid technology that DaimlerChrysler calls "Through-The-Road" (TTR). Instead of coupling the gasoline engine and electric motor/generator with a shaft, the engineers designed the system so that the road on which the vehicle runs acts almost like a belt connecting the two parts of the powertrain. The TTR system also provides 4-wheel drive functionality without the efficiency penalties of a conventional transfer case.

In the Durango HEV, a V-6 engine and automatic transmission connect to a conventional drive shaft that turns the rear wheels. A three-phase electric motor drives the front wheels, laying extra power on the pavement to assist the gasoline engine during acceleration. When the vehicle is decelerating, the motor regenerates braking energy from the front wheels. If the battery charge gets too low, the control system switches the motor into generator mode while the vehicle is cruising. The resulting drag on the road pulls extra power out of the gasoline engine—another aspect of the Through-The-Road coupling that gives the system its name. DaimlerChrysler has also shown European concept versions of this TTR hybrid system for two Mercedes-Benz models. The "HyPer" applies hybrid technology to a Mercedes A-Class car, and the "Hymatic" is based on a Mercedes E-Class sedan.

DaimlerChrysler's other announced hybrid is the Contractor Special, to be offered as an option for Dodge Ram full-size pickup trucks starting in 2004. This hybrid design is different than the company's

Slated for model year 2003, the hybrid-electric Dodge Durango TTR (Through-The-Road) uses pavement between the wheels to couple its electric motor and 3.9-liter gasoline engine.

Photo: DaimlerChrysler Corp.

TTR configuration. Its electric motor is mounted between the transmission and the transfer case of a 4x4 truck. The motor will provide extra power for acceleration and double as a generator to supply electric power. In this regard, it is similar to GM's planned Silverado/Sierra hybrids. When parked, the Contractor Special's hybrid components can function as a stationary electrical generator, delivering up to 20 kW of 110/220 volt AC power for worksite, campsite, or home uses.

However, the Dodge Contractor Special has a different design emphasis than GM's announced hybrid pickups. Its hybrid system will be used for boosting the performance of the gasoline engine, not just for recovering braking energy and providing auxiliary power. DaimlerChrysler plans to build these hybrid variants of the Ram to provide higher fuel efficiency and lower emissions as well as superior performance. For example, the 5.2-liter gas-electric motor hybrid will do 0–60 mph in 10.0 seconds while having a rated fuel efficiency of 18 MPG, compared to a 10.6 second 0–60 time and 16 MPG for the 5.9-liter gasoline-only models.

Greener Tech Tomorrow

The hybrid vehicles now on the market and soon to be introduced are but the firstborn in a "baby boom" of next-generation automotive design. Increasing electronic smarts as well as a move toward drivetrain

Ford's aluminum-intensive P2000 concept car weighs in at 2,000 pounds, 40 percent lighter than a conventional midsize car. *Photo: Ford Motor Company and Wieck Photo DataBase, Inc.*

electrification are just some of the traits of this new wave of technology. As seen in the Toyota Prius, Honda Insight, and other pioneering models, other traits of the new generation include extra-efficient and super-clean engines as well as advances in materials and vehicle structures. A key "insight" is that future green vehicle designs will encompass many innovations, not just a single "silver bullet" like electric drive.

Big strides in efficiency can be made by cutting vehicle mass through the use of lighter, high-strength steels, lightweight metals such as aluminum and magnesium, and advanced plastics and composites. An aluminum-based structure, as used on the Honda Insight for example, cuts weight substantially compared to standard stamped steel body while improving rigidity and crashworthiness.

An important opportunity is the prospect of building lighter-weight SUVs. Safety as well as environmental concerns dictate that it is the heaviest vehicles that need to lose weight first and most. Ford has built a research fleet of aluminum-based midsize cars that tip the scales at 2,000 pounds, 40 percent less than today's typical 3,300 pound curb weight. They then extended that approach to develop an aluminum-intensive SUV body that is 50 percent lighter that of today's Ford Explorer. This degree of weight reduction improves efficiency no matter what kind of engine is used and makes hybrid drivetrains more affordable.

The internal combustion engine still has some years of improvement ahead. Advanced engine technologies abound. Variable valve control is exemplified by Honda's VTEC (first introduced in 1989),

The Toyota eCom and DaimlerChrysler GEM are but two of the new battery-powered electric minicars being explored for use in community settings. *Photos: Toyota Motor Sales, U.S.A. and DaimlerChrysler Corp.*

Toyota's VVT-i, BMW's VANOS, and most recently GM's cam-phasing VVT (as used on a new inline six for the Chevy Trailblazer). Optimized versions of this engine refinement offer up to a 10–15 percent efficiency boost while aiding emissions control. A host of other techniques exist for reducing energy-wasting friction, cutting the weight of the engine and its accessories, and improving air induction. A combination of cleaner gasoline, advanced catalysts, and electronic controls can cut gasoline engine pollution to near-zero levels.

Electric Minicars

Pure electric cars, relying only on stored battery power and plugging in to recharge, do not have great prospects as general-purpose vehicles, but they could become increasingly handy in emerging market segments. Examples include neighborhood vehicles for serving transit stations or short-distance commuting in cities. The electric vehicles listed in our tables are still very costly for their size and have limited range, even though they do provide great "green" performance. The state of California is hoping to expand the market for battery electric cars through its zero-emission vehicle (ZEV) mandate and financial incentives.

One future option might be electric minicars, which are being explored in station car demonstration projects or for use in certain community settings. For instance, Honda is developing a concept called "ICVS," for Intelligent Community Vehicle Systems, that integrates a minicar within a specially designed landscape. Other examples include the DaimlerChrysler GEM, Ford Th!nk City, Nissan Hypermini, and Toyota eCom. Ford, for example, has been conducting consumer tests of the European version of its Th!nk City in preparation for U.S. sales and leasing of an enhanced version of the car that will meet both U.S. and European safety standards.

DaimlerChrysler's NECAR 5 represents another step along the path to practical fuel cell cars, which may be the ultimate in environmentally friendly vehicle design.

Photo: DaimlerChrysler Corp.

Fuel Cell Vehicles

Looking farther down the road, perhaps the most promising "Greener Tech" of tomorrow is the fuel cell. Fuel cells are like batteries in that they convert chemical energy directly into electricity. But they have the big advantage of being able to do this from an onboard fuel, ideally hydrogen. Fuel cells have powered many space missions, but recent research breakthroughs have cut their costs down to where mainstream uses now look feasible. Fuel cell buses have already been demonstrated in actual transit service. A number of automakers now have drivable fuel cell test cars, and other companies have shown concepts or are working toward the construction of fuel cell demonstration fleets. The California Fuel Cell Partnership is working to put test fleets of fuel cell cars into demonstration service over the next 2–3 years.

However, it is unclear if and when fuel cell vehicles will become widely available. Part of the reason is that costs still need to drop considerably. Also, a lot of new engineering is needed to make the components of a fuel cell engine work reliably in the challenging confines and changing conditions experienced by cars and trucks. Even if the necessary breakthroughs occur and good engineering progress is made, it will probably be 15 years before fuel cells become viable for truly mass-market cars and light trucks.

Perhaps the biggest barrier is getting the right fuel to the cells.

Nearly all fuel cells, and particularly those that would work well in vehicles, need pure hydrogen gas to operate. Hydrogen is difficult to store, and widespread distribution for it does not exist. Car companies are exploring more convenient fuels, such as gasoline or alcohols, but these add cost and complexity to the fuel cell powertrain while detracting from its efficiency. Buses present a better near-term opportunity for fuel cells, since they have more onboard space, can fill up at depots, and tolerate higher costs than automobiles.

Hooking up to alternative fuel supplies and converting various fuels to hydrogen are much lower barriers to the use of fuel cells in stationary electric power generation and even small electronic devices. Cost hurdles may also be less severe in non-automotive applications. So, fuels cells may be providing electricity to offices and factories some years before they become common under your car's hood.

Green buyers should be cheered by the fact that low-pollution piston engines still have great potential in the years ahead. Improvements in bodies, interiors, engines, and transmissions, along with the added benefit of hybrid drive, promise a steady stream of efficiency gains and pollution reduction from gasoline cars and trucks. Such progress can benefit the health of both people and the planet at relatively low cost, and sooner rather than later. In short, much of the "Greener Tech" we need tomorrow is already somewhere on the road today.

Green Ratings
for 2002 Vehicles

SAMPLE LISTING AND KEY TO *ACEEE'S GREEN BOOK™*

Emission Standard.

Federal certification:

Tier 1	Current national standard.
Tier 1-D	National standard for diesels.
HDT	Heavy Duty Truck

California certification:

TLEV	Transitional-Low-Emission Vehicle
LEV	Low-Emission Vehicle
ULEV	Ultra-Low-Emission Vehicle
SULEV	Super-Ultra-Low-Emission Vehicle
ZEV	Zero-Emission Vehicle

Manufacturer and model.

Fuel Economy, City and **Hwy.** City and highway fuel economy in miles per gallon (MPG), adjusted to reflect real-world driving conditions according to an EPA formula.

Values for Compressed Natural Gas (CNG) vehicles are in equivalent-MPG. Values for electric vehicles are in miles per kilowatt-hour (mi/kWh).

	Emission Standard	Fuel Economy City	Hwy
ACURA MDX 3.5L 6, auto 4wd [P]	ULEV	17	23

Number of Cylinders.

Engine Displacement. Specified in liters (L).

Transmission. Manual, automatic, or "auto stk" (manually adjustable automatic transmissions such as Tiptronic® or AutoStick®). A few vehicles have continuously variable automatic transmissions, indicated by CVT.

Fuel Type. All vehicles use regular gasoline unless indicated by:

[P]	Premium Gasoline
[D]	Diesel
[CNG]	Compressed Natural Gas
Electric	Electric Vehicle
FFV	Flexible Fuel Vehicle

Note: Automakers use a variety of trimline designations, such as "DX," "LX," "SS," etc., on their vehicles, but their meaning is not uniform across makes and models. Therefore, *ACEEE's Green Book™* relies on engine and transmission specifications to distinguish among models.

Class Ranking. This symbol compares vehicles *within the same class.*

Shaded Listings. Denote vehicles with likely limited availability. See page 7 for details.

Fuel Cost/yr. Estimated annual fuel costs based on 15,000 miles of driving and national average fuel prices.

✔ Superior
▲ Above Average
○ Average
▽ Below Average
✖ Inferior

Health Cost/yr. Estimated annual health costs from pollution based on damage cost estimates and emissions of CO, HC, NO_x and PM. This value represents the annual cost imposed on society due to illnesses and premature deaths in proportion to the amount of pollution produced by the vehicle.

Note: No vehicle gets a superior (✔) rating if its Green Score is worse than the average for all 2002 vehicles, even if it is the best in its class.

Fuel Cost/yr	Health Cost/yr	GHG tons/yr	EDX ¢/mile	Green Score	Class Ranking
$1,300	$160	14	2.48	22	▲

GHG tons/yr. Tons of CO_2 and other greenhouse gasses (GHG) emitted per year. Other GHGs are weighted according to their global warming impact. For example, a pound of methane has the same impact as about 22 pounds of CO_2.

Green Score. The EDX is converted to a 0-100 Green Score scale, where 100 represents the ideal of a pollution-free vehicle. The Green Score can be used to compare vehicles across different classes.

EDX ¢/mile. The Environmental Damage Index represents a vehicle's overall environmental impact. The EDX is expressed as the environmental cost to society from each mile the vehicle travels (in cents per mile), accounting for both health costs and global warming.

	Emission Standard	Fuel Economy City	Fuel Economy Hwy	Fuel Cost/yr	Health Cost/yr	GHG tons/yr	EDX ¢/mi	Green Score	Class Ranking
TWO SEATERS									
ACURA NSX									
3.0L 6, auto stk [P]	LEV	17	24	$1,240	$140	13	2.29	**24**	▽
3.2L 6, manual [P]	LEV	17	24	$1,300	$140	13	2.31	**24**	▽
ASTON MARTIN VANQUISH									
5.9L 12, auto stk [P]	LEV	12	19	$1,650	$170	17	2.92	**17**	✖
AUDI TT ROADSTER									
1.8L 4, manual [P]	LEV	22	31	$950	$130	10	1.91	**30**	▲
AUDI TT ROADSTER QUATTRO									
1.8L 4, manual 4wd [P]	TLEV	20	28	$1,080	$150	11	2.15	**26**	○
BMW M COUPE									
3.2L 6, manual [P]	LEV	17	25	$1,240	$140	13	2.27	**24**	○
BMW M ROADSTER									
3.2L 6, manual [P]	LEV	17	25	$1,240	$140	13	2.27	**24**	○
BMW Z3 COUPE									
3.0L 6, manual [P]	ULEV	21	29	$1,030	$120	11	1.88	**30**	▲
3.0L 6, auto [P]	ULEV	19	27	$1,130	$130	12	2.04	**28**	○
BMW Z3 ROADSTER									
3.0L 6, manual [P]	ULEV	21	29	$1,030	$120	11	1.88	**30**	▲
2.5L 6, manual [P]	LEV	20	27	$1,080	$130	11	2.02	**28**	○
3.0L 6, auto [P]	ULEV	19	25	$1,180	$120	12	2.05	**27**	○
2.5L 6, auto stk [P]	LEV	19	26	$1,130	$130	12	2.07	**27**	○
BMW Z8									
4.9L 8, manual [P]	TLEV	13	21	$1,550	$180	16	2.84	**18**	✖
CHEVROLET CORVETTE									
5.7L 8, manual [P]	LEV	19	28	$1,130	$130	12	2.09	**27**	○
5.7L 8, auto [P]	LEV	18	25	$1,180	$140	12	2.22	**25**	○
CHRYSLER PROWLER									
3.5L 6, auto stk	Tier 1	18	23	$1,130	$160	13	2.35	**23**	▽
FERRARI 360 MODENA/SPIDER									
3.6L 8, manual [P]	LEV	11	16	$1,900	$190	19	3.23	**15**	✖
3.6L 8, auto stk [P]	LEV	10	16	$2,060	$190	19	3.26	**14**	✖
FORD THUNDERBIRD									
3.9L 8, auto [P]	LEV	17	23	$1,300	$150	13	2.39	**23**	▽

See pages 64-65 for explanation of data and symbols.

	Emission Standard	Fuel Economy City	Fuel Economy Hwy	Fuel Cost/yr	Health Cost/yr	GHG tons/yr	EDX ¢/mi	Green Score	Class Ranking
TWO SEATERS (cont.)									
HONDA INSIGHT									
1.0L 3, auto CVT	SULEV	57	56	$400	$50	5	0.84	**57**	✔
1.0L 3, manual	ULEV	61	68	$350	$70	5	0.92	**54**	✔
1.0L 3, manual	LEV	61	68	$350	$80	5	0.98	**52**	✔
1.0L 3, auto CVT	LEV	57	56	$400	$80	5	1.08	**49**	✔
HONDA S2000									
2.0L 4, manual [P]	LEV	20	26	$1,080	$130	11	2.01	**28**	○
LAMBORGHINI L-147 MURCIELAGO									
6.2L 12, manual 4wd [P]	Tier 1	9	13	$2,480	$240	23	3.94	**10**	✖
6.2L 12, manual 4wd [P]	Tier 1	9	13	$2,480	$240	23	3.94	**10**	✖
MAZDA MX-5 MIATA									
1.8L 4, manual [P]	LEV	23	28	$990	$120	10	1.83	**31**	▲
1.8L 4, auto [P]	LEV	22	28	$1,030	$120	10	1.89	**30**	▲
MERCEDES-BENZ SL500									
5.0L 8, auto [P]	LEV	16	23	$1,300	$160	14	2.47	**22**	▽
MERCEDES-BENZ SL600									
6.0L 12, auto [P]	Tier 1	13	19	$1,650	$200	17	3.04	**16**	✖
MERCEDES-BENZ SLK230 KOMPRESSOR									
2.3L 4, auto [P]	LEV	23	30	$990	$130	10	1.92	**30**	▲
2.3L 4, manual [P]	LEV	20	30	$1,030	$130	11	1.97	**29**	○
MERCEDES-BENZ SLK32 AMG									
3.2L 6, auto [P]	LEV	18	24	$1,240	$140	12	2.22	**25**	○
MERCEDES-BENZ SLK320									
3.2L 6, auto [P]	LEV	20	26	$1,130	$130	12	2.09	**27**	○
3.2L 6, manual [P]	LEV	17	26	$1,240	$140	13	2.26	**25**	○
PORSCHE 911 GT2									
3.6L 6, manual [P]	LEV	15	22	$1,380	$150	14	2.48	**22**	▽
PORSCHE BOXSTER									
2.7L 6, manual [P]	LEV	19	27	$1,130	$130	11	2.04	**28**	○
2.7L 6, auto stk [P]	LEV	17	25	$1,240	$140	12	2.20	**25**	○
PORSCHE BOXSTER S									
3.2L 6, manual [P]	LEV	18	26	$1,240	$140	12	2.17	**26**	○
3.2L 6, auto stk [P]	LEV	17	25	$1,240	$140	13	2.29	**24**	▽
TOYOTA MR2									
1.8L 4, manual	LEV	25	30	$830	$110	9	1.72	**33**	▲

See pages 64-65 for explanation of data and symbols.

	Emission Standard	Fuel Economy City Hwy		Fuel Cost/yr	Health Cost/yr	GHG tons/yr	EDX ¢/mi	Green Score	Class Ranking

SUBCOMPACT CARS

ACURA RSX
2.0L 4, manual	LEV	27	33	$780	$110	9	1.70	**34**	▲
2.0L 4, auto stk	LEV	24	33	$830	$120	10	1.77	**32**	○
2.0L 4, manual [P]	LEV	24	31	$920	$120	10	1.78	**32**	○

AUDI TT COUPE
1.8L 4, manual [P]	LEV	23	31	$950	$120	10	1.83	**31**	○

AUDI TT COUPE QUATTRO
1.8L 4, manual 4wd [P]	LEV	20	29	$1,030	$130	11	2.01	**28**	○
1.8L 4, manual 4wd [P]	TLEV	20	28	$1,080	$150	11	2.15	**26**	▽

BENTLEY AZURE
6.8L 8, auto [P]	Tier 1	11	16	$1,900	$230	20	3.59	**12**	✖

BENTLEY CONTINENTAL SC
6.8L 8, auto [P]	Tier 1	11	16	$1,900	$230	20	3.58	**12**	✖

BENTLEY CONTINENTAL T
6.8L 8, auto [P]	Tier 1	11	16	$1,900	$230	20	3.58	**12**	✖

BMW 325Ci
2.5L 6, manual [P]	LEV	20	29	$1,030	$130	11	2.01	**28**	○
2.5L 6, auto stk [P]	LEV	19	27	$1,130	$140	12	2.12	**27**	○

BMW 325Ci CONVERTIBLE
2.5L 6, manual [P]	LEV	19	27	$1,130	$140	12	2.19	**25**	▽
2.5L 6, auto stk [P]	LEV	19	26	$1,180	$140	12	2.22	**25**	▽

BMW 330Ci
3.0L 6, manual [P]	ULEV	21	30	$1,030	$120	11	1.93	**30**	○
3.0L 6, auto [P]	ULEV	19	27	$1,130	$130	12	2.04	**28**	○

BMW 330Ci CONVERTIBLE
3.0L 6, manual [P]	ULEV	20	28	$1,080	$130	12	2.06	**27**	○
3.0L 6, auto [P]	ULEV	18	26	$1,180	$140	12	2.19	**25**	▽

BMW M3
3.2L 6, manual [P]	LEV	16	24	$1,300	$150	13	2.35	**23**	✖

BMW M3 CONVERTIBLE
3.2L 6, manual [P]	LEV	16	23	$1,380	$150	14	2.46	**22**	✖

See pages 64-65 for explanation of data and symbols.

	Emission Standard	Fuel Economy City Hwy		Fuel Cost/yr	Health Cost/yr	GHG tons/yr	EDX ¢/mi	Green Score	Class Ranking

SUBCOMPACT CARS (cont.)

CHEVROLET CAMARO
3.8L 6, manual	LEV	19	31	$980	$130	11	2.05	**28**	○
3.8L 6, auto	LEV	19	30	$980	$130	11	2.05	**28**	○
5.7L 8, manual [P]	LEV	19	28	$1,130	$130	12	2.09	**27**	○
5.7L 8, auto [P]	LEV	18	25	$1,180	$140	12	2.22	**25**	▽

FORD ESCORT ZX2
2.0L 4, manual	LEV	26	33	$780	$110	9	1.68	**34**	▲
2.0L 4, auto	LEV	25	33	$800	$110	9	1.72	**33**	▲

FORD MUSTANG
3.8L 6, manual	ULEV	20	29	$980	$120	11	1.99	**29**	○
3.8L 6, auto	ULEV	19	27	$1,020	$130	12	2.04	**28**	○
3.8L 6, manual	LEV	20	29	$980	$130	11	2.05	**28**	○
3.8L 6, auto	LEV	19	27	$1,020	$130	12	2.10	**27**	○
4.6L 8, manual	TLEV	18	26	$1,070	$150	12	2.30	**24**	✖
4.6L 8, auto	TLEV	17	24	$1,130	$160	13	2.38	**23**	✖

HONDA CIVIC HX
1.7L 4, manual	ULEV	36	44	$580	$90	7	1.32	**42**	✔
1.7L 4, auto CVT	ULEV	35	40	$610	$90	7	1.36	**41**	✔

JAGUAR XK8
4.0L 8, auto [P]	LEV	17	24	$1,240	$150	13	2.33	**24**	✖

JAGUAR XK8 CONVERTIBLE
4.0L 8, auto [P]	LEV	17	24	$1,240	$150	13	2.33	**24**	✖

JAGUAR XKR
4.0L 8, auto [P]	Tier 1	16	22	$1,300	$170	14	2.56	**21**	✖

JAGUAR XKR CONVERTIBLE
4.0L 8, auto [P]	Tier 1	16	22	$1,300	$170	14	2.56	**21**	✖

LEXUS SC 430
4.3L 8, auto [P]	ULEV	18	23	$1,240	$140	13	2.25	**25**	▽

MERCEDES-BENZ CLK320
3.2L 6, auto [P]	LEV	20	27	$1,080	$130	11	2.08	**27**	○

MERCEDES-BENZ CLK320 CABRIOLET
3.2L 6, auto [P]	LEV	19	26	$1,130	$140	12	2.18	**26**	▽

See pages 64-65 for explanation of data and symbols.

	Emission Standard	Fuel Economy City Hwy	Fuel Cost/yr	Health Cost/yr	GHG tons/yr	EDX ¢/mi	Green Score	Class Ranking
SUBCOMPACT CARS (cont.)								
MERCEDES-BENZ CLK430								
4.3L 8, auto [P]	ULEV	18 24	$1,240	$130	13	2.19	**25**	▽
MERCEDES-BENZ CLK430 CABRIOLET								
4.3L 8, auto [P]	ULEV	17 24	$1,240	$140	13	2.27	**24**	▽
MERCEDES-BENZ CLK55 AMG								
5.4L 8, auto [P]	LEV	17 24	$1,240	$150	13	2.32	**24**	✖
MERCEDES-BENZ CLK55 AMG CABRIOLET								
5.4L 8, auto [P]	LEV	16 22	$1,380	$150	14	2.45	**22**	✖
MITSUBISHI ECLIPSE								
2.4L 4, manual	LEV	23 30	$900	$120	10	1.86	**31**	○
3.0L 6, manual [P]	LEV	20 28	$1,080	$130	11	2.04	**28**	○
2.4L 4, auto	LEV	20 27	$980	$130	11	2.06	**27**	○
3.0L 6, auto stk [P]	LEV	20 28	$1,080	$130	11	2.07	**27**	○
2.4L 4, auto stk	LEV	20 27	$1,020	$130	11	2.08	**27**	○
MITSUBISHI ECLIPSE SPYDER								
2.4L 4, manual	LEV	22 29	$900	$130	11	1.95	**29**	○
3.0L 6, manual [P]	LEV	20 29	$1,080	$130	11	2.04	**28**	○
3.0L 6, auto stk [P]	LEV	19 28	$1,130	$130	12	2.08	**27**	○
2.4L 4, auto stk	LEV	20 26	$1,020	$130	12	2.10	**27**	○
MITSUBISHI MIRAGE								
1.5L 4, manual	LEV	32 39	$640	$100	8	1.46	**39**	✔
1.8L 4, manual	LEV	29 36	$700	$100	8	1.55	**37**	✔
1.5L 4, auto	LEV	28 35	$730	$110	8	1.59	**36**	▲
1.8L 4, auto	LEV	26 32	$800	$110	9	1.70	**34**	▲
PONTIAC FIREBIRD								
3.8L 6, manual	LEV	19 31	$980	$130	11	2.05	**28**	○
3.8L 6, auto	LEV	19 30	$980	$130	11	2.05	**28**	○
5.7L 8, manual [P]	LEV	19 28	$1,130	$140	12	2.19	**25**	▽
5.7L 8, auto [P]	LEV	18 26	$1,180	$140	12	2.25	**25**	▽
PORSCHE 911 CARRERA								
3.6L 6, auto stk [P]	LEV	18 26	$1,180	$140	12	2.19	**25**	▽
3.6L 6, manual [P]	LEV	18 26	$1,180	$140	12	2.20	**25**	▽
PORSCHE 911 CARRERA 4 CABRIOLET								
3.6L 6, manual 4wd [P]	LEV	17 24	$1,300	$140	13	2.31	**24**	✖
3.6L 6, auto stk 4wd [P]	LEV	17 23	$1,300	$140	13	2.32	**24**	✖

See pages 64-65 for explanation of data and symbols.

	Emission Standard	Fuel Economy City	Fuel Economy Hwy	Fuel Cost/yr	Health Cost/yr	GHG tons/yr	EDX ¢/mi	Green Score	Class Ranking
SUBCOMPACT CARS (cont.)									
PORSCHE 911 CARRERA 4S									
3.6L 6, manual 4wd [P]	LEV	17	24	$1,300	$140	13	2.31	**24**	✖
3.6L 6, auto stk 4wd [P]	LEV	17	23	$1,300	$140	13	2.32	**24**	✖
PORSCHE 911 CARRERA CABRIOLET									
3.6L 6, auto stk [P]	LEV	18	26	$1,180	$140	12	2.19	**25**	▽
3.6L 6, manual [P]	LEV	18	26	$1,180	$140	12	2.20	**25**	▽
PORSCHE 911 TARGA									
3.6L 6, auto stk [P]	LEV	18	26	$1,180	$140	12	2.19	**25**	▽
3.6L 6, manual [P]	LEV	18	26	$1,180	$140	12	2.20	**25**	▽
PORSCHE 911 TURBO									
3.6L 6, manual 4wd [P]	LEV	15	22	$1,380	$150	14	2.48	**22**	✖
3.6L 6, auto stk 4wd [P]	LEV	15	22	$1,460	$150	14	2.51	**21**	✖
ROLLS-ROYCE CORNICHE									
6.8L 8, auto [P]	Tier 1	11	16	$1,900	$230	20	3.59	**12**	✖
SAAB 9-3 CONVERTIBLE									
2.0L 4, manual [P]	LEV	23	33	$950	$120	10	1.87	**31**	○
2.0L 4, auto [P]	LEV	21	29	$1,030	$130	11	1.99	**28**	○
SAAB 9-3 VIGGEN CONVERTIBLE									
2.3L 4, manual [P]	LEV	19	28	$1,130	$130	12	2.09	**27**	○
SATURN SC									
1.9L 4, manual	LEV	28	40	$680	$100	8	1.52	**37**	✔
1.9L 4, manual	LEV	27	38	$730	$110	9	1.61	**36**	▲
1.9L 4, auto	LEV	26	36	$780	$110	9	1.66	**35**	▲
1.9L 4, auto	LEV	25	36	$780	$110	9	1.67	**34**	▲
SUBARU IMPREZA 2.5 RS SEDAN									
2.5L 4, manual Awd	LEV	20	28	$980	$130	11	1.99	**29**	○
2.5L 4, auto Awd	LEV	22	27	$940	$130	11	1.99	**29**	○
SUBARU IMPREZA WRX SEDAN									
2.0L 4, manual Awd [P]	LEV	20	27	$1,080	$130	11	2.06	**27**	○
2.0L 4, auto Awd [P]	LEV	19	26	$1,130	$140	12	2.12	**27**	○
SUZUKI ESTEEM									
1.8L 4, manual	LEV	28	35	$730	$110	8	1.58	**36**	▲
1.6L 4, auto	LEV	27	34	$750	$110	9	1.61	**35**	▲
1.8L 4, auto	LEV	26	33	$780	$110	9	1.68	**34**	▲

See pages 64-65 for explanation of data and symbols.

	Emission Standard	Fuel Economy City	Hwy	Fuel Cost/yr	Health Cost/yr	GHG tons/yr	EDX ¢/mi	Green Score	Class Ranking

SUBCOMPACT CARS (cont.)

TOYOTA CAMRY SOLARA CONVERTIBLE

2.4L 4, auto	ULEV	23	31	$870	$120	10	1.84	31	○
3.0L 6, auto	LEV	19	26	$1,070	$140	12	2.20	25	▽

TOYOTA CELICA

1.8L 4, auto	TLEV	29	36	$730	$120	8	1.69	34	▲
1.8L 4, manual	TLEV	28	33	$750	$130	9	1.74	33	▲
1.8L 4, manual [P]	TLEV	23	32	$950	$130	10	1.90	30	○
1.8L 4, auto stk [P]	TLEV	23	30	$950	$140	10	1.95	29	○

VOLKSWAGEN CABRIO

2.0L 4, manual	LEV	24	31	$830	$120	10	1.78	32	○
2.0L 4, auto	LEV	23	29	$900	$120	10	1.87	31	○

VOLKSWAGEN NEW BEETLE

2.0L 4, manual	ULEV	24	31	$830	$110	10	1.72	33	▲
2.0L 4, manual	LEV	24	31	$830	$120	10	1.78	32	○
1.8L 4, manual [P]	LEV	24	31	$920	$120	10	1.79	32	○
2.0L 4, auto	ULEV	23	29	$900	$110	10	1.81	32	○
1.8L 4, auto [P]	LEV	23	29	$990	$120	10	1.86	31	○
2.0L 4, auto	LEV	23	29	$900	$120	10	1.87	31	○
1.8L 4, manual [P]	LEV	23	30	$950	$130	10	1.90	30	○
1.9L 4, manual [D]	TIER 1-D	42	49	$480	$250	6	2.31	24	✖
1.9L 4, auto [D]	TIER 1-D	34	44	$570	$260	7	2.43	22	✖

VOLVO C70 CONVERTIBLE

2.3L 5, manual [P]	LEV	21	27	$1,080	$140	11	2.09	27	○
2.4L 5, auto [P]	LEV	20	27	$1,080	$140	11	2.10	27	○
2.3L 5, auto [P]	LEV	20	26	$1,130	$140	12	2.16	26	▽

See pages 64-65 for explanation of data and symbols.

	Emission Standard	Fuel Economy City	Fuel Economy Hwy	Fuel Cost/yr	Health Cost/yr	GHG tons/yr	EDX ¢/mi	Green Score	Class Ranking
COMPACT CARS									
ACURA 3.2CL									
3.2L 6, auto stk [P]	ULEV	19	29	$1,080	$120	11	1.99	**28**	○
3.2L 6, auto stk [P]	LEV	19	29	$1,080	$130	11	2.06	**27**	▽
ACURA 3.2CL TYPE-S									
3.2L 6, auto stk [P]	LEV	19	29	$1,080	$140	12	2.11	**27**	▽
AUDI A4									
1.8L 4, manual [P]	ULEV	22	31	$990	$120	10	1.85	**31**	○
1.8L 4, auto CVT [P]	ULEV	20	29	$1,080	$120	11	1.96	**29**	○
3.0L 6, auto CVT [P]	ULEV	19	27	$1,130	$130	12	2.09	**27**	▽
AUDI A4 QUATTRO									
1.8L 4, manual 4wd [P]	ULEV	21	29	$1,030	$120	11	1.94	**29**	○
1.8L 4, auto 4wd [P]	ULEV	19	28	$1,130	$130	12	2.08	**27**	▽
3.0L 6, manual 4wd [P]	ULEV	18	25	$1,240	$140	13	2.23	**25**	✖
3.0L 6, auto 4wd [P]	ULEV	17	25	$1,240	$140	13	2.24	**25**	✖
AUDI S4									
2.7L 6, manual 4wd [P]	TLEV	17	23	$1,240	$160	13	2.45	**22**	✖
2.7L 6, auto stk 4wd [P]	TLEV	17	24	$1,240	$160	13	2.45	**22**	✖
BENTLEY CONTINENTAL R									
6.8L 8, auto [P]	Tier 1	11	16	$1,900	$230	20	3.58	**12**	✖
BMW 325i									
2.5L 6, manual [P]	LEV	20	29	$1,030	$130	11	2.01	**28**	○
2.5L 6, auto stk [P]	LEV	19	27	$1,130	$140	12	2.12	**27**	▽
BMW 325xi									
2.5L 6, manual 4wd [P]	LEV	19	27	$1,130	$130	12	2.09	**27**	▽
2.5L 6, auto stk 4wd [P]	LEV	19	26	$1,180	$140	12	2.22	**25**	✖
BMW 330i									
3.0L 6, manual [P]	ULEV	21	30	$1,030	$120	11	1.93	**30**	○
3.0L 6, auto [P]	ULEV	19	27	$1,130	$130	12	2.04	**28**	○
BMW 330xi									
3.0L 6, manual 4wd [P]	LEV	20	27	$1,080	$140	12	2.13	**26**	▽
3.0L 6, auto 4wd [P]	LEV	17	25	$1,240	$150	13	2.31	**24**	✖
BMW 525i									
2.5L 6, manual [P]	LEV	20	29	$1,030	$130	11	2.01	**28**	○
2.5L 6, auto stk [P]	LEV	19	27	$1,130	$140	12	2.12	**27**	▽

See pages 64-65 for explanation of data and symbols.

	Emission Standard	Fuel Economy City	Hwy	Fuel Cost/yr	Health Cost/yr	GHG tons/yr	EDX ¢/mi	Green Score	Class Ranking
COMPACT CARS (cont.)									
BMW 530i									
3.0L 6, manual [P]	ULEV	21	30	$1,030	$120	11	1.93	**30**	○
3.0L 6, auto [P]	ULEV	18	26	$1,180	$140	12	2.19	**25**	▽
BMW 540i									
4.4L 8, auto [P]	LEV	18	24	$1,240	$150	13	2.29	**24**	✖
4.4L 8, manual [P]	LEV	15	23	$1,380	$150	14	2.49	**22**	✖
4.4L 8, auto stk [P]	LEV	15	21	$1,460	$160	14	2.55	**21**	✖
BMW M5									
4.9L 8, manual [P]	TLEV	13	21	$1,550	$180	16	2.84	**18**	✖
CHEVROLET CAVALIER¹									
2.2L 4, manual	LEV	25	33	$800	$120	9	1.75	**33**	○
2.2L 4, auto	LEV	24	32	$830	$120	10	1.78	**32**	○
2.2L 4, manual	TLEV	24	33	$830	$130	10	1.86	**31**	○
2.4L 4, manual	LEV	22	32	$900	$120	10	1.87	**31**	○
2.4L 4, auto	LEV	21	28	$940	$130	11	1.96	**29**	○
CHEVROLET PRIZM									
1.8L 4, manual	LEV	32	41	$640	$100	8	1.47	**39**	▲
1.8L 4, auto	LEV	30	40	$660	$100	8	1.51	**38**	▲
1.8L 4, auto	LEV	29	33	$730	$110	9	1.61	**35**	▲
CHRYSLER SEBRING CONVERTIBLE									
2.4L 4, auto	LEV	21	30	$940	$130	11	1.98	**29**	○
2.7L 6, auto	LEV	20	27	$1,020	$140	12	2.14	**26**	▽
2.7L 6, auto stk	LEV	19	27	$1,020	$140	12	2.16	**26**	▽
CHRYSLER SEBRING COUPE									
2.4L 4, manual	LEV	22	29	$900	$130	11	1.95	**29**	○
2.4L 4, auto	LEV	21	28	$940	$130	11	2.01	**28**	○
3.0L 6, manual	LEV	20	29	$980	$130	11	2.04	**28**	○
3.0L 6, auto	LEV	20	28	$980	$130	11	2.06	**27**	▽
3.0L 6, auto stk	LEV	20	28	$980	$130	11	2.07	**27**	▽
DAEWOO LANOS									
1.5L 4, manual	TLEV	26	36	$750	$130	9	1.75	**33**	○
1.5L 4, auto	TLEV	24	37	$800	$130	9	1.82	**31**	○

See pages 64-65 for explanation of data and symbols.
¹ *A compressed natural gas (CNG)-gasoline bi-fuel version of this vehicle is also available.*

	Emission Standard	Fuel Economy City	Hwy	Fuel Cost/yr	Health Cost/yr	GHG tons/yr	EDX ¢/mi	Green Score	Class Ranking
COMPACT CARS (cont.)									
DAEWOO NUBIRA									
2.0L 4, manual	LEV	22	31	$900	$120	10	1.86	**31**	○
2.0L 4, auto	LEV	22	31	$900	$120	10	1.88	**30**	○
2.0L 4, manual	TLEV	22	31	$900	$140	10	1.97	**29**	○
2.0L 4, auto	TLEV	22	31	$900	$140	10	1.98	**29**	○
DODGE NEON									
2.0L 4, manual	LEV	28	34	$750	$110	9	1.62	**35**	▲
2.0L 4, auto	LEV	24	31	$830	$120	10	1.78	**32**	○
DODGE STRATUS COUPE									
2.4L 4, manual	LEV	22	29	$900	$130	11	1.95	**29**	○
2.4L 4, auto	LEV	21	28	$940	$130	11	2.01	**28**	○
3.0L 6, manual	LEV	20	29	$980	$130	11	2.04	**28**	○
3.0L 6, auto	LEV	20	28	$980	$130	11	2.06	**27**	▽
3.0L 6, auto stk	LEV	20	28	$980	$130	11	2.07	**27**	▽
FORD ESCORT									
2.0L 4, auto	LEV	26	35	$780	$110	9	1.66	**34**	▲
FORD FOCUS									
2.0L 4, manual	ULEV	28	36	$730	$100	8	1.56	**37**	▲
2.0L 4, manual	LEV	28	36	$730	$110	9	1.62	**35**	▲
2.0L 4, manual	ULEV	25	34	$780	$110	9	1.65	**35**	▲
2.0L 4, auto	ULEV	26	32	$800	$110	9	1.66	**34**	▲
2.0L 4, auto	LEV	26	32	$800	$110	9	1.72	**33**	○
HONDA CIVIC									
1.7L 4, manual	ULEV	33	39	$630	$90	8	1.40	**40**	✔
1.7L 4, manual	ULEV	32	37	$660	$100	8	1.45	**39**	✔
1.7L 4, auto	ULEV	31	38	$660	$100	8	1.46	**39**	✔
1.7L 4, auto	ULEV	30	38	$680	$100	8	1.48	**38**	▲
2.0L 4, manual	LEV	26	30	$800	$120	9	1.74	**33**	○
HONDA CIVIC GX									
1.7L 4, auto CVT [CNG][2]	SULEV	30	34	$660	$40	7	0.98	**52**	✔
HYUNDAI ACCENT									
1.5L 4, manual	LEV	28	36	$730	$110	8	1.57	**36**	▲
1.6L 4, manual	LEV	27	37	$730	$110	9	1.61	**35**	▲
1.6L 4, auto	LEV	25	35	$780	$110	9	1.69	**34**	▲
1.5L 4, auto	LEV	25	35	$780	$110	9	1.69	**34**	▲

See pages 64-65 for explanation of data and symbols.
[2] *CNG fuel economy is given as gasoline-equivalent MPG.*

	Emission Standard	Fuel Economy City Hwy	Fuel Cost/yr	Health Cost/yr	GHG tons/yr	EDX ¢/mi	Green Score	Class Ranking
COMPACT CARS (cont.)								
HYUNDAI ELANTRA								
2.0L 4, manual	ULEV	25 33	$800	$110	9	1.69	**34**	▲
2.0L 4, auto	ULEV	24 33	$800	$110	9	1.69	**34**	▲
2.0L 4, manual	LEV	25 33	$800	$120	9	1.75	**33**	○
2.0L 4, auto	LEV	24 33	$800	$120	9	1.76	**33**	○
INFINITI G20								
2.0L 4, manual	LEV	24 31	$830	$120	10	1.81	**32**	○
2.0L 4, auto	LEV	23 30	$870	$120	10	1.84	**31**	○
JAGUAR X-TYPE								
2.5L 6, manual 4wd [P]	LEV	19 28	$1,130	$140	12	2.14	**26**	▽
2.5L 6, auto 4wd [P]	LEV	19 26	$1,130	$140	12	2.20	**25**	▽
3.0L 6, manual 4wd [P]	LEV	18 28	$1,130	$140	12	2.20	**25**	▽
3.0L 6, auto 4wd [P]	LEV	18 25	$1,180	$140	13	2.26	**24**	✖
JAGUAR XJ SPORT								
4.0L 8, auto [P]	LEV	17 24	$1,240	$150	13	2.33	**24**	✖
JAGUAR XJ8								
4.0L 8, auto [P]	LEV	17 24	$1,240	$150	13	2.33	**24**	✖
JAGUAR XJR								
4.0L 8, auto [P]	Tier 1	16 22	$1,380	$180	14	2.68	**20**	✖
KIA RIO								
1.5L 4, manual	LEV	27 32	$780	$110	9	1.68	**34**	▲
1.5L 4, auto	LEV	25 30	$830	$110	9	1.74	**33**	○
KIA SPECTRA								
1.8L 4, manual	ULEV	24 32	$830	$110	10	1.74	**33**	○
1.8L 4, auto	ULEV	22 30	$900	$110	10	1.84	**31**	○
LEXUS IS 300								
3.0L 6, manual [P]	LEV	18 25	$1,180	$140	12	2.22	**25**	✖
3.0L 6, auto stk [P]	LEV	18 25	$1,240	$140	12	2.22	**25**	✖
MAZDA MILLENIA								
2.5L 6, auto [P]	TLEV	20 27	$1,130	$150	12	2.21	**25**	✖
2.3L 6, auto [P]	Tier 1	20 28	$1,130	$150	12	2.21	**25**	✖
MAZDA PROTEGE/PROTEGE5								
2.0L 4, manual	ULEV	25 31	$830	$110	9	1.71	**34**	▲
2.0L 4, auto	ULEV	25 30	$830	$110	10	1.73	**33**	○

See pages 64-65 for explanation of data and symbols.

	Emission Standard	Fuel Economy City	Fuel Economy Hwy	Fuel Cost/yr	Health Cost/yr	GHG tons/yr	EDX ¢/mi	Green Score	Class Ranking

COMPACT CARS (cont.)

MERCEDES-BENZ C230 KOMPRESSOR
2.3L 4, auto [P]	LEV	21	28	$1,030	$130	11	1.99	28	○
2.3L 4, manual [P]	LEV	19	29	$1,130	$130	12	2.08	27	▽

MERCEDES-BENZ C240
2.6L 6, auto [P]	LEV	19	26	$1,130	$140	12	2.12	26	▽
2.6L 6, manual [P]	LEV	17	26	$1,240	$140	13	2.24	25	✖

MERCEDES-BENZ C32 AMG
3.2L 6, auto [P]	LEV	17	22	$1,300	$150	13	2.40	23	✖

MERCEDES-BENZ C320
3.2L 6, auto [P]	LEV	19	25	$1,130	$140	12	2.14	26	▽

MERCEDES-BENZ CL500
5.0L 8, auto [P]	ULEV	16	23	$1,300	$150	14	2.43	22	✖

MERCEDES-BENZ CL55 AMG
5.4L 8, auto [P]	LEV	16	22	$1,380	$160	14	2.52	21	✖

MERCEDES-BENZ CL600
5.8L 12, auto [P]	TLEV	15	22	$1,460	$180	15	2.73	19	✖

MERCURY COUGAR
2.0L 4, manual	TLEV	23	34	$830	$130	10	1.89	30	○
2.5L 6, manual	TLEV	21	30	$940	$150	11	2.10	27	▽
2.5L 6, auto	TLEV	20	29	$980	$150	11	2.15	26	▽

MITSUBISHI LANCER
1.6L 4, manual	LEV	28	33	$750	$110	9	1.64	35	▲
2.0L 4, manual	LEV	26	33	$800	$110	9	1.72	33	○
1.6L 4, auto	LEV	24	29	$870	$120	10	1.78	32	○
2.0L 4, auto	LEV	24	30	$870	$120	10	1.82	31	○

NISSAN SENTRA
1.8L 4, manual	ULEV	27	35	$730	$100	9	1.55	37	▲
1.8L 4, auto	ULEV	27	33	$750	$100	9	1.58	36	▲
2.5L 4, manual	ULEV	24	29	$870	$110	10	1.78	32	○
2.5L 4, auto	ULEV	23	28	$900	$110	10	1.84	31	○
2.5L 4, manual	LEV	22	28	$940	$120	11	1.91	30	○

NISSAN SENTRA CA
1.8L 4, auto	SULEV	27	33	$750	$80	9	1.40	40	✔

See pages 64-65 for explanation of data and symbols.

	Emission Standard	Fuel Economy City Hwy	Fuel Cost/yr	Health Cost/yr	GHG tons/yr	EDX ¢/mi	Green Score	Class Ranking

COMPACT CARS (cont.)

OLDSMOBILE ALERO

2.2L 4, manual	LEV	25 33	$800	$120	9	1.75	**33**	○
2.2L 4, auto	LEV	24 32	$830	$120	10	1.78	**32**	○
3.4L 6, auto	LEV	21 32	$900	$130	11	1.93	**29**	○

PONTIAC GRAND AM

2.2L 4, manual	LEV	25 33	$800	$120	9	1.75	**33**	○
2.2L 4, auto	LEV	24 32	$830	$120	10	1.78	**32**	○
3.4L 6, auto	LEV	21 32	$900	$130	11	1.93	**29**	○

PONTIAC SUNFIRE

2.2L 4, manual	LEV	25 33	$800	$120	9	1.75	**33**	○
2.2L 4, auto	LEV	24 32	$830	$120	10	1.78	**32**	○
2.4L 4, manual	LEV	22 32	$900	$120	10	1.87	**31**	○
2.2L 4, manual	TLEV	23 33	$830	$130	10	1.90	**30**	○
2.4L 4, auto	LEV	21 28	$940	$130	11	1.96	**29**	○

SATURN SL

1.9L 4, manual	LEV	29 40	$680	$100	8	1.51	**38**	▲
1.9L 4, auto	LEV	27 37	$730	$110	8	1.58	**36**	▲
1.9L 4, manual	LEV	27 38	$730	$110	9	1.61	**36**	▲
1.9L 4, auto	LEV	25 36	$780	$110	9	1.67	**34**	▲

SUBARU LEGACY SEDAN

2.5L 4, auto Awd	LEV	22 27	$940	$130	11	1.99	**28**	○
2.5L 4, manual Awd	LEV	21 27	$980	$130	11	2.03	**28**	○

SUBARU OUTBACK SEDAN

2.5L 4, auto Awd	LEV	22 27	$940	$130	11	1.99	**28**	○
3.0L 6, auto Awd [P]	LEV	20 26	$1,130	$140	12	2.16	**26**	▽

TOYOTA CAMRY SOLARA

2.4L 4, manual	ULEV	24 33	$830	$110	10	1.76	**33**	○
2.4L 4, auto	ULEV	23 32	$830	$110	10	1.80	**32**	○
3.0L 6, auto	LEV	20 27	$1,020	$130	12	2.10	**27**	▽
3.0L 6, manual	Tier 1	20 27	$1,020	$150	12	2.22	**25**	✖

TOYOTA COROLLA

1.8L 4, manual	LEV	32 41	$630	$100	8	1.47	**39**	▲
1.8L 4, auto	LEV	30 39	$660	$100	8	1.52	**37**	▲
1.8L 4, auto	LEV	29 33	$730	$110	9	1.61	**35**	▲

See pages 64-65 for explanation of data and symbols.

	Emission Standard	Fuel Economy City	Hwy	Fuel Cost/yr	Health Cost/yr	GHG tons/yr	EDX ¢/mi	Green Score	Class Ranking
COMPACT CARS (cont.)									
TOYOTA ECHO									
1.5L 4, manual	LEV	34	41	$610	$100	7	1.38	**41**	✔
1.5L 4, auto	LEV	32	38	$640	$100	8	1.46	**39**	▲
TOYOTA PRIUS									
1.5L 4, auto CVT	SULEV	52	45	$470	$60	6	1.01	**51**	✔
1.5L 4, auto CVT	ULEV	52	45	$470	$80	6	1.18	**46**	✔
VOLKSWAGEN GOLF									
2.0L 4, manual	ULEV	24	31	$830	$110	10	1.72	**33**	○
2.0L 4, manual	LEV	24	31	$830	$120	10	1.78	**32**	○
2.0L 4, auto	ULEV	23	29	$900	$110	10	1.81	**32**	○
2.0L 4, auto	LEV	23	29	$900	$120	10	1.87	**31**	○
1.9L 4, manual [D]	TIER 1-D	42	49	$480	$250	6	2.31	**24**	✖
1.9L 4, auto [D]	TIER 1-D	34	45	$570	$260	7	2.48	**22**	✖
VOLKSWAGEN GTI									
1.8L 4, manual [P]	LEV	24	31	$920	$120	10	1.79	**32**	○
1.8L 4, auto stk [P]	LEV	22	29	$990	$130	11	1.95	**29**	○
2.8L 6, manual	LEV	20	28	$980	$130	11	1.99	**29**	○
VOLKSWAGEN JETTA									
2.0L 4, manual	ULEV	24	31	$830	$110	10	1.72	**33**	○
2.0L 4, manual	LEV	24	31	$830	$120	10	1.78	**32**	○
2.0L 4, auto	ULEV	23	29	$900	$110	10	1.81	**32**	○
1.8L 4, manual [P]	LEV	24	31	$920	$120	10	1.85	**31**	○
2.0L 4, auto	LEV	23	29	$900	$120	10	1.87	**31**	○
1.8L 4, auto stk [P]	LEV	22	29	$990	$130	11	1.95	**29**	○
2.8L 6, manual	LEV	19	28	$980	$130	11	2.08	**27**	▽
2.8L 6, auto	LEV	19	26	$1,070	$140	12	2.16	**26**	▽
1.9L 4, manual [D]	TIER 1-D	42	49	$480	$250	6	2.31	**24**	✖
1.9L 4, auto [D]	TIER 1-D	34	45	$570	$260	7	2.48	**22**	✖
VOLKSWAGEN PASSAT 4MOTION									
2.8L 6, auto stk 4wd [P]	LEV	19	26	$1,130	$140	12	2.20	**25**	▽
VOLVO C70 COUPE									
2.3L 5, auto [P]	LEV	21	29	$1,030	$130	11	2.01	**28**	○
2.3L 5, manual [P]	LEV	20	27	$1,080	$130	11	2.06	**27**	▽
VOLVO S40									
1.9L 4, auto [P]	LEV	22	30	$990	$130	11	1.96	**29**	○

See pages 64-65 for explanation of data and symbols.

	Emission Standard	Fuel Economy City	Hwy	Fuel Cost/yr	Health Cost/yr	GHG tons/yr	EDX ¢/mi	Green Score	Class Ranking

COMPACT CARS (cont.)

VOLVO S60

2.4L 5, manual [P]	ULEV	21	28	$1,030	$120	11	1.94	**29**	○
2.4L 5, auto [P]	ULEV	21	28	$1,030	$120	11	1.94	**29**	○
2.3L 5, auto stk [P]	LEV	21	29	$1,030	$130	11	2.01	**28**	○
2.4L 5, auto [P]	LEV	21	28	$1,080	$130	11	2.02	**28**	○
2.3L 5, manual [P]	LEV	20	27	$1,080	$130	11	2.06	**27**	▽
2.4L 5, auto stk Awd [P]	LEV	19	26	$1,130	$140	12	2.17	**26**	▽

SMALL WAGONS

AUDI S4 AVANT

2.7L 6, manual 4wd [P]	TLEV	17	23	$1,240	$160	13	2.45	**22**	✖
2.7L 6, auto stk 4wd [P]	TLEV	17	24	$1,240	$160	13	2.45	**22**	✖

BMW 325i SPORT WAGON

2.5L 6, manual [P]	LEV	20	29	$1,030	$130	11	2.01	**28**	○
2.5L 6, auto stk [P]	LEV	19	27	$1,130	$140	12	2.12	**27**	▽

BMW 325xi SPORT WAGON

2.5L 6, manual 4wd [P]	LEV	19	26	$1,130	$140	12	2.19	**26**	▽
2.5L 6, auto stk 4wd [P]	LEV	19	26	$1,180	$140	12	2.22	**25**	▽

BMW 525i SPORT WAGON

2.5L 6, manual [P]	LEV	19	27	$1,130	$140	12	2.19	**25**	▽
2.5L 6, auto stk [P]	LEV	19	26	$1,180	$140	12	2.22	**25**	▽

BMW 540i SPORT WAGON

4.4L 8, auto stk [P]	LEV	15	21	$1,460	$160	14	2.55	**21**	✖

CHRYSLER PT CRUISER

2.4L 4, manual	LEV	21	29	$940	$130	11	1.98	**29**	○
2.4L 4, auto	ULEV	19	25	$1,020	$130	12	2.07	**27**	○
2.4L 4, auto	LEV	19	25	$1,020	$140	12	2.13	**26**	▽

DAEWOO NUBIRA WAGON

2.0L 4, manual	LEV	22	31	$900	$120	10	1.86	**31**	▲
2.0L 4, auto	LEV	22	31	$900	$120	10	1.88	**30**	▲
2.0L 4, manual	TLEV	22	31	$900	$140	10	1.97	**29**	○
2.0L 4, auto	TLEV	22	31	$900	$140	10	1.98	**29**	○

See pages 64-65 for explanation of data and symbols.

	Emission Standard	Fuel Economy City	Hwy	Fuel Cost/yr	Health Cost/yr	GHG tons/yr	EDX ¢/mi	Green Score	Class Ranking
SMALL WAGONS (cont.)									
MERCEDES-BENZ C320 WAGON									
3.2L 6, auto [P]	LEV	19	25	$1,180	$140	12	2.21	**25**	▽
SUBARU IMPREZA 2.5 TS SPORT WAGON									
2.5L 4, auto Awd	LEV	22	27	$940	$130	11	1.99	**29**	○
2.5L 4, manual Awd	LEV	21	27	$980	$130	11	2.03	**28**	○
SUBARU IMPREZA OUTBACK SPORT									
2.5L 4, auto Awd	LEV	22	27	$940	$130	11	1.99	**29**	○
2.5L 4, manual Awd	LEV	21	27	$980	$130	11	2.03	**28**	○
SUBARU IMPREZA WRX SPORT WAGON									
2.0L 4, manual Awd [P]	LEV	20	27	$1,080	$130	11	2.06	**27**	○
2.0L 4, auto Awd [P]	LEV	19	26	$1,130	$140	12	2.12	**27**	▽
SUZUKI ESTEEM WAGON									
1.8L 4, manual	LEV	27	34	$750	$110	9	1.64	**35**	✔
1.6L 4, auto	LEV	26	33	$780	$110	9	1.68	**34**	✔
1.8L 4, auto	LEV	26	33	$780	$110	9	1.68	**34**	✔
VOLKSWAGEN JETTA WAGON									
2.0L 4, manual	ULEV	24	31	$830	$110	10	1.79	**32**	▲
1.8L 4, manual [P]	LEV	24	31	$920	$120	10	1.85	**31**	▲
2.0L 4, manual	LEV	24	31	$830	$120	10	1.85	**31**	▲
2.0L 4, auto	ULEV	22	29	$900	$120	10	1.88	**30**	▲
2.0L 4, auto	LEV	22	29	$900	$130	11	1.94	**29**	○
1.8L 4, auto stk [P]	LEV	22	29	$990	$130	11	1.95	**29**	○
2.8L 6, manual	LEV	19	28	$980	$130	11	2.08	**27**	○
2.8L 6, auto	LEV	19	26	$1,070	$140	12	2.16	**26**	▽
1.9L 4, manual [D]	TIER 1-D	42	50	$480	$260	6	2.35	**23**	✖
1.9L 4, auto [D]	TIER 1-D	34	45	$570	$260	7	2.48	**22**	✖
VOLVO V40									
1.9L 4, auto [P]	LEV	22	30	$990	$130	11	1.96	**29**	○

See pages 64-65 for explanation of data and symbols.

	Emission Standard	Fuel Economy City	Hwy	Fuel Cost/yr	Health Cost/yr	GHG tons/yr	EDX ¢/mi	Green Score	Class Ranking

MIDSIZE CARS

ACURA 3.2TL

3.2L 6, auto stk [P]	ULEV	19	29	$1,080	$120	11	1.99	**28**	○
3.2L 6, auto stk [P]	LEV	19	29	$1,080	$130	11	2.06	**27**	○

ACURA 3.5RL

3.5L 6, auto [P]	LEV	18	24	$1,240	$150	13	2.32	**24**	▽

AUDI A6

3.0L 6, auto CVT [P]	ULEV	19	25	$1,180	$130	12	2.16	**26**	○

AUDI A6 QUATTRO

3.0L 6, auto 4wd [P]	ULEV	17	25	$1,240	$140	13	2.24	**25**	▽
4.2L 8, auto stk 4wd [P]	LEV	17	25	$1,240	$150	13	2.33	**24**	✖
2.7L 6, manual 4wd [P]	TLEV	17	24	$1,240	$160	13	2.44	**22**	✖
2.7L 6, auto stk 4wd [P]	TLEV	17	24	$1,240	$160	13	2.45	**22**	✖

AUDI A8 QUATTRO

4.2L 8, auto stk 4wd [P]	LEV	17	25	$1,240	$150	13	2.33	**24**	✖

AUDI S8 QUATTRO

4.2L 8, auto stk 4wd [P]	TLEV	15	21	$1,460	$180	15	2.71	**19**	✖

BENTLEY ARNAGE

6.8L 8, auto [P]	Tier 1	11	16	$1,900	$230	20	3.58	**12**	✖

BUICK CENTURY

3.1L 6, auto	LEV	20	29	$980	$130	11	2.04	**28**	○

BUICK REGAL

3.8L 6, auto	ULEV	19	29	$980	$120	11	2.01	**28**	○
3.8L 6, auto	LEV	19	29	$980	$130	11	2.07	**27**	○
3.8L 6, auto [P]	LEV	18	27	$1,180	$140	12	2.24	**25**	▽

CADILLAC ELDORADO

4.6L 8, auto	LEV	18	27	$1,070	$140	12	2.26	**25**	▽

CADILLAC SEVILLE

4.6L 8, auto	LEV	18	27	$1,070	$140	12	2.26	**25**	▽

CHEVROLET MALIBU

3.1L 6, auto	LEV	20	29	$980	$130	11	2.04	**28**	○

See pages 64-65 for explanation of data and symbols.

	Emission Standard	Fuel Economy City	Hwy	Fuel Cost/yr	Health Cost/yr	GHG tons/yr	EDX ¢/mi	Green Score	Class Ranking
MIDSIZE CARS (cont.)									
CHEVROLET MONTE CARLO									
3.4L 6, auto	LEV	21	32	$900	$130	11	1.93	**29**	▲
3.8L 6, auto	ULEV	19	29	$980	$120	11	2.01	**28**	○
3.8L 6, auto	LEV	19	29	$980	$130	11	2.07	**27**	○
CHRYSLER SEBRING SEDAN									
2.4L 4, auto	LEV	21	30	$940	$130	11	1.98	**29**	○
2.7L 6, auto	LEV	20	28	$980	$130	11	2.05	**28**	○
2.7L 6, auto stk	LEV	20	27	$980	$130	11	2.06	**27**	○
DAEWOO LEGANZA									
2.2L 4, manual	LEV	20	28	$980	$130	11	2.04	**28**	○
2.2L 4, auto	LEV	20	28	$980	$130	11	2.08	**27**	○
2.2L 4, manual	TLEV	20	28	$980	$150	11	2.15	**26**	○
2.2L 4, auto	TLEV	20	28	$980	$150	12	2.19	**25**	▽
DODGE STRATUS SEDAN									
2.4L 4, auto	LEV	21	30	$940	$130	11	1.98	**29**	○
2.7L 6, auto	LEV	20	28	$980	$130	11	2.05	**28**	○
2.7L 6, auto stk	LEV	20	27	$980	$130	11	2.06	**27**	○
HONDA ACCORD									
2.3L 4, auto	SULEV	23	30	$870	$90	10	1.66	**34**	✔
2.3L 4, manual	ULEV	26	32	$800	$110	10	1.73	**33**	✔
2.3L 4, manual	LEV	25	32	$830	$120	10	1.77	**32**	▲
2.3L 4, manual	LEV	26	32	$800	$120	10	1.80	**32**	▲
2.3L 4, auto	ULEV	23	30	$870	$120	10	1.84	**31**	▲
2.3L 4, auto	LEV	23	30	$870	$130	10	1.90	**30**	▲
3.0L 6, auto	LEV	20	28	$980	$130	11	2.04	**28**	○
HYUNDAI SONATA									
2.4L 4, manual	LEV	22	30	$900	$130	10	1.91	**30**	▲
2.4L 4, auto	LEV	22	30	$900	$130	11	1.95	**29**	▲
2.7L 6, manual	LEV	20	27	$980	$130	11	2.06	**27**	○
2.7L 6, auto	LEV	20	27	$980	$130	11	2.06	**27**	○
HYUNDAI XG350									
3.5L 6, auto	LEV	18	26	$1,070	$140	13	2.26	**24**	▽
INFINITI I35									
3.5L 6, auto	LEV	20	26	$1,020	$130	12	2.10	**27**	○

See pages 64-65 for explanation of data and symbols.

83

	Emission Standard	Fuel Economy City	Hwy	Fuel Cost/yr	Health Cost/yr	GHG tons/yr	EDX ¢/mi	Green Score	Class Ranking

MIDSIZE CARS (cont.)

INFINITI Q45

| 4.5L 8, auto stk [P] | TLEV | 17 | 25 | $1,240 | $160 | 13 | 2.42 | 22 | ✖ |

JAGUAR S-TYPE

| 3.0L 6, auto [P] | LEV | 18 | 25 | $1,240 | $150 | 13 | 2.28 | 24 | ▽ |
| 4.0L 8, auto [P] | LEV | 17 | 24 | $1,240 | $150 | 13 | 2.33 | 24 | ✖ |

JAGUAR SUPER V8

| 4.0L 8, auto [P] | Tier 1 | 16 | 22 | $1,380 | $180 | 14 | 2.68 | 20 | ✖ |

JAGUAR VANDEN PLAS

| 4.0L 8, auto [P] | LEV | 17 | 24 | $1,240 | $150 | 13 | 2.33 | 24 | ✖ |

KIA OPTIMA

2.4L 4, manual	LEV	21	28	$940	$130	11	2.00	28	○
2.4L 4, auto	LEV	20	27	$1,020	$130	12	2.09	27	○
2.7L 6, manual	LEV	19	26	$1,070	$140	12	2.17	26	○
2.7L 6, auto	LEV	18	24	$1,130	$140	12	2.23	25	▽

LEXUS ES 300

| 3.0L 6, auto | ULEV | 21 | 29 | $940 | $120 | 11 | 1.94 | 29 | ▲ |

LEXUS GS 300

| 3.0L 6, auto stk [P] | LEV | 18 | 25 | $1,180 | $140 | 12 | 2.25 | 25 | ▽ |

LEXUS GS 430

| 4.3L 8, auto [P] | ULEV | 18 | 23 | $1,240 | $140 | 13 | 2.25 | 25 | ▽ |

LEXUS LS 430

| 4.3L 8, auto [P] | ULEV | 18 | 25 | $1,180 | $140 | 12 | 2.19 | 25 | ▽ |

LINCOLN LS

3.0L 6, auto [P]	LEV	18	25	$1,180	$140	13	2.26	25	▽
3.0L 6, auto stk [P]	LEV	17	24	$1,240	$150	13	2.35	23	✖
3.0L 6, manual [P]	TLEV	18	25	$1,180	$160	13	2.36	23	✖
3.9L 8, auto [P]	LEV	17	23	$1,300	$150	13	2.39	23	✖
3.9L 8, auto stk [P]	LEV	17	24	$1,300	$150	13	2.39	23	✖

MAZDA 626

2.0L 4, manual	ULEV	26	32	$780	$110	9	1.66	35	✔
2.0L 4, auto	ULEV	22	28	$940	$120	11	1.87	31	▲
2.5L 6, manual [P]	TLEV	21	27	$1,080	$150	11	2.14	26	○
2.5L 6, auto [P]	TLEV	20	26	$1,130	$150	12	2.19	25	▽

See pages 64-65 for explanation of data and symbols.

	Emission Standard	Fuel Economy City Hwy	Fuel Cost/yr	Health Cost/yr	GHG tons/yr	EDX ¢/mi	Green Score	Class Ranking

MIDSIZE CARS (cont.)

MERCEDES-BENZ E320

3.2L 6, auto [P]	ULEV	20 28	$1,080	$130	11	2.03	**28**	○

MERCEDES-BENZ E320 4MATIC

3.2L 6, auto 4wd [P]	ULEV	20 27	$1,130	$130	12	2.08	**27**	○

MERCEDES-BENZ E430

4.3L 8, auto [P]	ULEV	17 24	$1,240	$140	13	2.25	**25**	▽

MERCEDES-BENZ E430 4MATIC

4.3L 8, auto 4wd [P]	ULEV	17 23	$1,300	$140	13	2.30	**24**	▽

MERCEDES-BENZ E55 AMG

5.4L 8, auto [P]	LEV	17 24	$1,240	$150	13	2.34	**23**	✖

MERCURY SABLE[3]

3.0L 6, auto	LEV	20 28	$980	$130	11	2.05	**27**	○
3.0L 6, auto	LEV	20 27	$980	$130	11	2.07	**27**	○

MITSUBISHI DIAMANTE

3.5L 6, auto [P]	LEV	18 25	$1,240	$150	13	2.29	**24**	▽

MITSUBISHI GALANT

2.4L 4, auto	ULEV	21 28	$940	$120	11	1.95	**29**	▲
2.4L 4, auto	LEV	21 28	$940	$130	11	2.01	**28**	○
3.0L 6, auto [P]	LEV	20 27	$1,130	$130	11	2.08	**27**	○

NISSAN ALTIMA

2.5L 4, manual	ULEV	23 29	$870	$120	10	1.83	**31**	▲
2.5L 4, auto	ULEV	23 29	$900	$120	10	1.86	**31**	▲
3.5L 6, manual	LEV	21 26	$980	$130	11	2.04	**28**	○
3.5L 6, auto	LEV	19 26	$1,070	$140	12	2.15	**26**	○

NISSAN MAXIMA

3.5L 6, manual	LEV	21 28	$940	$130	11	2.00	**28**	○
3.5L 6, auto	LEV	20 26	$1,020	$130	12	2.10	**27**	○

OLDSMOBILE AURORA

3.5L 6, auto	LEV	18 27	$1,070	$140	12	2.23	**25**	▽
4.0L 8, auto	LEV	18 26	$1,070	$140	12	2.25	**25**	▽

OLDSMOBILE INTRIGUE

3.5L 6, auto	LEV	20 30	$940	$130	11	2.00	**28**	○

See pages 64-65 for explanation of data and symbols.
[3] *An ethanol-gasoline flex-fuel version of this vehicle is also available.*

	Emission Standard	Fuel Economy City Hwy	Fuel Cost/yr	Health Cost/yr	GHG tons/yr	EDX ¢/mi	Green Score	Class Ranking

MIDSIZE CARS (cont.)

PONTIAC GRAND PRIX
3.8L 6, auto	ULEV	19	29	$980	$120	11	2.01	28	○
3.1L 6, auto	LEV	20	29	$980	$130	11	2.04	28	○
3.8L 6, auto	LEV	19	29	$980	$130	11	2.07	27	○
3.8L 6, auto [P]	LEV	18	28	$1,180	$140	12	2.17	26	○

ROLLS-ROYCE SILVER SERAPH
5.4L 12, auto [P]	Tier 1	12	16	$1,770	$210	18	3.34	14	✖

SAAB 9-3
2.0L 4, manual [P]	LEV	23	33	$950	$120	10	1.87	31	▲
2.0L 4, auto [P]	LEV	21	29	$1,030	$130	11	1.99	28	○

SAAB 9-3 VIGGEN
2.3L 4, manual [P]	LEV	19	28	$1,130	$130	12	2.09	27	○

SAAB 9-5
2.3L 4, manual	LEV	22	31	$900	$130	11	1.93	29	▲
2.3L 4, manual [P]	LEV	21	31	$990	$130	11	1.95	29	▲
2.3L 4, auto [P]	LEV	20	30	$1,080	$140	11	2.08	27	○
2.3L 4, auto	LEV	20	29	$980	$140	12	2.11	27	○
3.0L 6, auto [P]	LEV	18	26	$1,180	$140	12	2.22	25	▽

SATURN L100/200
2.2L 4, manual	ULEV	25	33	$800	$110	9	1.68	34	✔
2.2L 4, auto	ULEV	24	33	$830	$110	10	1.72	33	✔

SATURN L300
3.0L 6, auto	LEV	21	29	$940	$130	11	2.01	28	○

TOYOTA CAMRY
2.4L 4, manual	ULEV	24	33	$830	$110	10	1.76	33	✔
2.4L 4, auto	ULEV	23	32	$830	$110	10	1.80	32	▲
3.0L 6, auto	ULEV	20	28	$980	$120	11	1.98	29	○

VOLKSWAGEN PASSAT
1.8L 4, manual [P]	ULEV	22	31	$990	$120	10	1.86	31	▲
1.8L 4, auto stk [P]	ULEV	21	30	$990	$120	11	1.89	30	▲
2.8L 6, manual [P]	LEV	20	28	$1,080	$130	11	2.06	27	○
2.8L 6, auto stk [P]	LEV	20	27	$1,130	$130	12	2.08	27	○

VOLVO S80
2.9L 6, auto [P]	ULEV	19	25	$1,130	$130	12	2.13	26	○

VOLVO S80 T6/EXECUTIVE
2.9L 6, auto stk [P]	ULEV	18	25	$1,180	$140	13	2.21	25	▽

See pages 64-65 for explanation of data and symbols.

	Emission Standard	Fuel Economy City	Hwy	Fuel Cost/yr	Health Cost/yr	GHG tons/yr	EDX ¢/mi	Green Score	Class Ranking
MIDSIZE WAGONS									
AUDI A6 AVANT QUATTRO									
3.0L 6, auto 4wd [P]	ULEV	17	25	$1,240	$140	13	2.24	**25**	▽
AUDI ALLROAD QUATTRO									
2.7L 6, manual 4wd [P]	TLEV	16	21	$1,380	$180	14	2.68	**20**	✖
2.7L 6, auto 4wd [P]	TLEV	15	21	$1,460	$180	15	2.73	**19**	✖
AUDI S6 AVANT									
4.2L 8, auto stk 4wd [P]	TLEV	14	21	$1,550	$190	16	2.88	**18**	✖
FORD FOCUS WAGON									
2.0L 4, manual	LEV	28	36	$730	$110	9	1.62	**35**	✔
2.0L 4, manual	ULEV	25	34	$780	$110	9	1.65	**35**	✔
2.0L 4, auto	ULEV	26	32	$800	$110	9	1.67	**34**	▲
2.0L 4, auto	LEV	26	32	$800	$110	9	1.73	**33**	▲
FORD TAURUS WAGON[4]									
3.0L 6, auto	LEV	20	26	$1,020	$140	12	2.15	**26**	○
3.0L 6, auto	LEV	19	26	$1,070	$140	12	2.20	**25**	▽
MERCEDES-BENZ E320 4MATIC WAGON									
3.2L 6, auto 4wd [P]	ULEV	19	26	$1,130	$130	12	2.11	**27**	○
MERCEDES-BENZ E320 WAGON									
3.2L 6, auto [P]	ULEV	20	27	$1,130	$130	12	2.08	**27**	○
MERCURY SABLE WAGON[5]									
3.0L 6, auto	LEV	20	26	$1,020	$140	12	2.15	**26**	○
3.0L 6, auto	LEV	19	26	$1,070	$140	12	2.20	**25**	▽
SAAB 9-5 WAGON									
2.3L 4, manual [P]	LEV	22	30	$990	$130	11	2.01	**28**	○
2.3L 4, manual	LEV	21	30	$900	$130	11	2.01	**28**	○
2.3L 4, auto [P]	LEV	20	28	$1,080	$140	12	2.13	**26**	○
2.3L 4, auto	LEV	19	28	$1,020	$140	12	2.15	**26**	○
3.0L 6, auto [P]	LEV	18	26	$1,180	$140	12	2.23	**25**	▽
SATURN LW200									
2.2L 4, manual	ULEV	24	32	$830	$110	10	1.77	**32**	▲
2.2L 4, auto	ULEV	24	33	$830	$110	10	1.77	**32**	▲
SATURN LW300									
3.0L 6, auto	LEV	21	29	$940	$130	11	2.01	**28**	○

See pages 64-65 for explanation of data and symbols.
[4/5] *An ethanol-gasoline flex-fuel version of this vehicle is also available.*

	Emission Standard	Fuel Economy City Hwy		Fuel Cost/yr	Health Cost/yr	GHG tons/yr	EDX ¢/mi	Green Score	Class Ranking
MIDSIZE WAGONS (cont.)									
SUBARU LEGACY WAGON									
2.5L 4, auto Awd	LEV	22	27	$940	$130	11	2.00	**28**	○
2.5L 4, manual Awd	LEV	21	27	$980	$130	11	2.03	**28**	○
SUBARU OUTBACK WAGON									
2.5L 4, auto Awd	LEV	22	27	$940	$130	11	2.00	**28**	○
2.5L 4, manual Awd	LEV	21	27	$980	$130	11	2.03	**28**	○
3.0L 6, auto Awd [P]	LEV	20	26	$1,130	$140	12	2.16	**26**	▽
VOLKSWAGEN PASSAT WAGON									
1.8L 4, manual [P]	ULEV	22	31	$990	$120	10	1.86	**31**	▲
1.8L 4, auto stk [P]	ULEV	21	30	$990	$120	11	1.89	**30**	▲
2.8L 6, manual [P]	LEV	20	28	$1,080	$130	11	2.06	**27**	○
2.8L 6, auto stk [P]	LEV	19	27	$1,130	$140	12	2.16	**26**	▽
VOLKSWAGEN PASSAT WAGON 4MOTION									
2.8L 6, auto stk 4wd [P]	LEV	19	26	$1,130	$140	12	2.20	**25**	▽
VOLVO CROSS COUNTRY									
2.4L 5, auto stk Awd [P]	LEV	19	25	$1,130	$160	12	2.30	**24**	✖
VOLVO V70									
2.4L 5, manual [P]	ULEV	21	28	$1,030	$120	11	1.94	**29**	○
2.4L 5, auto [P]	ULEV	21	28	$1,030	$120	11	1.94	**29**	○
2.3L 5, manual [P]	LEV	21	27	$1,080	$140	11	2.09	**27**	○
2.4L 5, auto [P]	LEV	20	27	$1,080	$140	11	2.10	**27**	○
2.3L 5, auto stk [P]	LEV	20	26	$1,130	$140	12	2.16	**26**	▽
2.4L 5, auto stk Awd [P]	LEV	19	26	$1,130	$140	12	2.17	**26**	▽
LARGE CARS									
AUDI A8 L									
4.2L 8, auto stk 4wd [P]	LEV	17	25	$1,240	$150	13	2.38	**23**	▽
BENTLEY ARNAGE LWB									
6.8L 8, auto [P]	Tier 1	11	16	$1,900	$230	20	3.58	**12**	✖
BMW 745i									
4.4L 8, auto [P]	LEV	18	26	$1,180	$150	13	2.30	**24**	▽
BMW 745Li									
4.4L 8, auto [P]	LEV	18	26	$1,180	$150	13	2.30	**24**	▽

See pages 64-65 for explanation of data and symbols.

	Emission Standard	Fuel Economy City	Fuel Economy Hwy	Fuel Cost/yr	Health Cost/yr	GHG tons/yr	EDX ¢/mi	Green Score	Class Ranking

LARGE CARS (cont.)

BUICK LESABRE
3.8L 6, auto	ULEV	20	29	$980	$130	11	2.05	28	▲
3.8L 6, auto	LEV	20	29	$980	$140	12	2.11	27	○

BUICK PARK AVENUE
3.8L 6, auto	ULEV	20	29	$980	$130	11	2.05	28	▲
3.8L 6, auto	LEV	20	29	$980	$140	12	2.11	27	○
3.8L 6, auto [P]	LEV	18	27	$1,180	$140	12	2.24	25	○

CADILLAC DEVILLE
4.6L 8, auto	LEV	18	27	$1,070	$140	12	2.26	25	○

CADILLAC LIMOUSINE
4.6L 8, auto	LEV	14	22	$1,320	$180	16	2.78	18	✖

CHEVROLET IMPALA
3.4L 6, auto	LEV	21	32	$900	$130	11	1.93	29	✔
3.8L 6, auto	ULEV	19	29	$980	$120	11	2.01	28	▲
3.8L 6, auto	LEV	19	29	$980	$130	11	2.07	27	○
3.8L 6, auto	LEV	18	28	$1,020	$140	12	2.19	25	○

CHRYSLER 300M
3.5L 6, auto stk	LEV	18	26	$1,070	$140	12	2.25	25	○

CHRYSLER CONCORDE
2.7L 6, auto	LEV	20	28	$980	$130	11	2.05	28	▲
3.5L 6, auto	LEV	18	26	$1,070	$140	12	2.23	25	○

DODGE INTREPID
2.7L 6, auto	LEV	20	28	$980	$130	11	2.05	28	▲
2.7L 6, auto stk	LEV	20	27	$980	$130	11	2.06	27	○
3.5L 6, auto	LEV	18	26	$1,070	$140	12	2.23	25	○
3.5L 6, auto stk	LEV	18	26	$1,070	$140	12	2.25	25	○

FORD CROWN VICTORIA
4.6L 8, auto [CNG][6]	ULEV	15	22	$1,170	$80	12	1.80	32	✔
4.6L 8, auto	LEV	17	25	$1,130	$150	13	2.32	24	▽
4.6L 8, auto	LEV	15	22	$1,250	$160	14	2.50	21	✖

FORD TAURUS[7]
3.0L 6, auto	LEV	20	28	$980	$130	11	2.05	27	○
3.0L 6, auto	LEV	20	27	$980	$130	11	2.07	27	○

See pages 64-65 for explanation of data and symbols.
[6] *CNG fuel economy is given as gasoline-equivalent MPG.*
[7] *An ethanol-gasoline flex-fuel version of this vehicle is also available.*

	Emission Standard	Fuel Economy City Hwy	Fuel Cost/yr	Health Cost/yr	GHG tons/yr	EDX ¢/mi	Green Score	Class Ranking

LARGE CARS (cont.)

LINCOLN CONTINENTAL

| 4.6L 8, auto [P] | TLEV | 17 25 | $1,240 | $160 | 13 | 2.42 | **22** | ▽ |

LINCOLN TOWN CAR

| 4.6L 8, auto | LEV | 17 23 | $1,180 | $150 | 14 | 2.44 | **22** | ▽ |

MERCEDES-BENZ S430

| 4.3L 8, auto [P] | ULEV | 17 24 | $1,240 | $140 | 13 | 2.34 | **23** | ▽ |

MERCEDES-BENZ S500

| 5.0L 8, auto [P] | ULEV | 16 23 | $1,300 | $150 | 14 | 2.43 | **22** | ▽ |

MERCEDES-BENZ S55 AMG

| 5.4L 8, auto [P] | LEV | 16 22 | $1,380 | $150 | 14 | 2.46 | **22** | ▽ |

MERCEDES-BENZ S600

| 5.8L 12, auto [P] | TLEV | 15 22 | $1,460 | $180 | 15 | 2.73 | **19** | ✖ |

MERCURY GRAND MARQUIS

| 4.6L 8, auto | LEV | 17 25 | $1,130 | $150 | 13 | 2.32 | **24** | ▽ |

PONTIAC BONNEVILLE

3.8L 6, auto	ULEV	20 29	$980	$130	11	2.05	**28**	▲
3.8L 6, auto	LEV	20 29	$980	$140	12	2.11	**27**	○
3.8L 6, auto [P]	LEV	18 27	$1,180	$140	12	2.24	**25**	○

ROLLS-ROYCE PARK WARD

| 5.4L 12, auto [P] | Tier 1 | 12 16 | $1,770 | $210 | 18 | 3.34 | **14** | ✖ |

TOYOTA AVALON

| 3.0L 6, auto | LEV | 21 29 | $940 | $130 | 11 | 1.97 | **29** | ✔ |

MINIVANS

CHEVROLET ASTRO (CARGO)

4.3L 6, auto	LEV	17 22	$1,180	$170	14	2.52	**21**	○
4.3L 6, auto Awd	LEV	15 20	$1,320	$180	15	2.79	**18**	▽
4.3L 6, auto Awd	Tier 1	15 20	$1,320	$210	15	2.96	**17**	✖

CHEVROLET ASTRO (PASSENGER)

4.3L 6, auto	LEV	15 20	$1,320	$180	15	2.76	**19**	▽
4.3L 6, auto Awd	ULEV	15 18	$1,410	$180	16	2.88	**18**	✖
4.3L 6, auto Awd	Tier 1	15 18	$1,410	$210	16	3.10	**16**	✖

See pages 64-65 for explanation of data and symbols.

	Emission Standard	Fuel Economy City Hwy	Fuel Cost/yr	Health Cost/yr	GHG tons/yr	EDX ¢/mi	Green Score	Class Ranking
MINIVANS (cont.)								
CHEVROLET VENTURE								
3.4L 6, auto	ULEV	19 26	$1,020	$150	12	2.24	**25**	✔
3.4L 6, auto	LEV	19 26	$1,020	$160	12	2.31	**24**	▲
3.4L 6, auto Awd	ULEV	18 24	$1,130	$160	13	2.41	**22**	○
3.4L 6, auto Awd	LEV	18 24	$1,130	$170	13	2.48	**22**	○
CHRYSLER TOWN & COUNTRY[8]								
3.3L 6, auto	LEV	18 24	$1,130	$160	13	2.44	**22**	○
3.8L 6, auto	LEV	18 24	$1,130	$170	13	2.51	**21**	○
3.8L 6, auto Awd	LEV	17 22	$1,180	$170	14	2.58	**21**	○
CHRYSLER VOYAGER[9]								
2.4L 4, auto	LEV	19 24	$1,070	$160	12	2.33	**24**	▲
3.3L 6, auto	LEV	18 24	$1,130	$160	13	2.44	**22**	○
DODGE CARAVAN[10]								
2.4L 4, auto	LEV	19 24	$1,070	$160	12	2.33	**24**	▲
3.3L 6, auto	LEV	18 24	$1,130	$160	13	2.44	**22**	○
3.8L 6, auto	LEV	18 24	$1,130	$170	13	2.51	**21**	○
3.8L 6, auto stk	LEV	17 24	$1,130	$170	14	2.52	**21**	○
3.8L 6, auto Awd	LEV	17 23	$1,180	$170	14	2.54	**21**	○
3.8L 6, auto stk Awd	LEV	17 23	$1,180	$170	14	2.57	**21**	○
FORD WINDSTAR VAN								
3.8L 6, auto	ULEV	17 23	$1,180	$160	13	2.42	**22**	○
FORD WINDSTAR WAGON								
3.8L 6, auto	ULEV	17 23	$1,180	$160	13	2.42	**22**	○
GMC SAFARI (CARGO)								
4.3L 6, auto	LEV	17 22	$1,180	$170	14	2.52	**21**	○
4.3L 6, auto Awd	ULEV	15 20	$1,320	$170	15	2.74	**19**	▽
4.3L 6, auto Awd	LEV	15 20	$1,320	$180	15	2.79	**18**	▽
4.3L 6, auto Awd	Tier 1	15 20	$1,320	$210	15	2.96	**17**	✖
GMC SAFARI (PASSENGER)								
4.3L 6, auto	LEV	15 20	$1,320	$180	15	2.76	**19**	▽
4.3L 6, auto Awd	ULEV	15 18	$1,410	$180	16	2.88	**18**	✖
4.3L 6, auto Awd	Tier 1	15 18	$1,410	$210	16	3.10	**16**	✖
HONDA ODYSSEY								
3.5L 6, auto	LEV	18 25	$1,070	$160	13	2.45	**22**	○

See pages 64-65 for explanation of data and symbols.
[8/9/10]*An ethanol-gasoline flex-fuel version of this vehicle is also available.*

	Emission Standard	Fuel Economy City	Hwy	Fuel Cost/yr	Health Cost/yr	GHG tons/yr	EDX ¢/mi	Green Score	Class Ranking
MINIVANS (cont.)									
KIA SEDONA									
3.5L 6, auto	LEV	15	20	$1,320	$180	15	2.83	**18**	▽
MAZDA MPV									
3.0L 6, auto	ULEV	18	24	$1,130	$150	13	2.36	**23**	▲
MERCURY VILLAGER									
3.3L 6, auto	LEV	17	23	$1,180	$170	14	2.55	**21**	○
NISSAN QUEST									
3.3L 6, auto	LEV	17	23	$1,180	$160	14	2.50	**21**	○
OLDSMOBILE SILHOUETTE									
3.4L 6, auto	ULEV	19	26	$1,020	$150	12	2.24	**25**	✔
3.4L 6, auto	LEV	19	26	$1,020	$160	12	2.31	**24**	▲
3.4L 6, auto Awd	ULEV	18	24	$1,130	$160	13	2.41	**22**	○
3.4L 6, auto Awd	LEV	18	24	$1,130	$170	13	2.48	**22**	○
PONTIAC MONTANA									
3.4L 6, auto	ULEV	19	26	$1,020	$150	12	2.24	**25**	✔
3.4L 6, auto	LEV	19	26	$1,020	$160	12	2.31	**24**	▲
3.4L 6, auto Awd	ULEV	18	24	$1,130	$160	13	2.41	**22**	○
3.4L 6, auto Awd	LEV	18	24	$1,130	$170	13	2.48	**22**	○
TOYOTA SIENNA									
3.0L 6, auto	LEV	19	24	$1,070	$160	13	2.35	**23**	▲
LARGE VANS									
CHEVROLET G1500/2500 EXPRESS[11]									
4.3L 6, auto	LEV	14	18	$1,410	$200	17	3.08	**16**	○
5.7L 8, auto	LEV	13	17	$1,500	$220	18	3.30	**14**	▽
5.0L 8, auto	Tier 1	14	18	$1,410	$250	17	3.39	**13**	▽
4.3L 6, auto	Tier 1	14	18	$1,410	$250	17	3.44	**13**	▽
5.7L 8, auto	Tier 1	13	17	$1,500	$260	18	3.56	**12**	✖
CHEVROLET G1500/2500 VAN									
4.3L 6, auto	LEV	15	18	$1,410	$190	16	2.96	**17**	○
5.0L 8, auto	Tier 1	15	19	$1,410	$210	16	3.10	**16**	○
4.3L 6, auto	Tier 1	15	18	$1,410	$220	16	3.11	**15**	○
5.7L 8, auto	LEV	14	17	$1,500	$210	17	3.20	**15**	○
5.7L 8, auto	Tier 1	14	17	$1,500	$250	17	3.45	**13**	✖

See pages 64-65 for explanation of data and symbols.

[11] *A compressed natural gas (CNG)-gasoline bi-fuel version of this vehicle is also available.*

	Emission Standard	Fuel Economy City	Hwy	Fuel Cost/yr	Health Cost/yr	GHG tons/yr	EDX ¢/mi	Green Score	Class Ranking

LARGE VANS (cont.)

DODGE RAM VAN 1500
3.9L 6, auto	Tier 1	14	16	$1,500	$220	17	3.17	**15**	○
5.9L 8, auto	ULEV	12	17	$1,610	$220	18	3.33	**14**	▽
5.9L 8, auto	Tier 1	12	17	$1,610	$230	18	3.43	**13**	▽

DODGE RAM VAN 2500
5.2L 8, auto [CNG][12]	SULEV	13	15	$980	$100	16	2.31	**24**	✔
5.2L 8, auto [CNG][13]	ULEV	13	15	$980	$130	16	2.53	**21**	▲
3.9L 6, auto	Tier 1	14	16	$1,500	$220	17	3.27	**14**	○
5.9L 8, auto	ULEV	12	17	$1,610	$220	18	3.33	**14**	▽
5.9L 8, auto	Tier 1	12	17	$1,610	$260	18	3.64	**12**	✖

DODGE RAM WAGON 1500
3.9L 6, auto	Tier 1	14	16	$1,500	$220	17	3.27	**14**	○

DODGE RAM WAGON 2500
5.2L 8, auto [CNG][14]	SULEV	13	15	$980	$110	16	2.36	**23**	✔
5.2L 8, auto [CNG][15]	ULEV	13	15	$980	$130	16	2.59	**20**	▲
5.9L 8, auto	ULEV	12	17	$1,610	$220	19	3.46	**13**	✖
5.9L 8, auto	Tier 1	12	17	$1,610	$270	19	3.77	**11**	✖

FORD E-150 CLUB WAGON
4.2L 6, auto	LEV	14	18	$1,410	$210	17	3.16	**15**	○
4.6L 8, auto	LEV	14	18	$1,500	$220	17	3.25	**14**	○
5.4L 8, auto	LEV	13	17	$1,500	$230	18	3.39	**13**	▽
4.2L 6, auto	Tier 1	14	18	$1,410	$250	17	3.42	**13**	▽

FORD E-150 ECONOLINE
4.6L 8, auto	LEV	15	20	$1,320	$200	15	2.94	**17**	○
4.2L 6, auto	LEV	14	18	$1,410	$190	16	3.00	**16**	○
5.4L 8, auto	LEV	15	19	$1,410	$210	16	3.03	**16**	○
4.2L 6, auto	Tier 1	14	18	$1,410	$220	17	3.16	**15**	○

FORD E-250 ECONOLINE
5.4L 8, auto [CNG][16]	SULEV	11	14	$1,120	$110	18	2.63	**20**	▲
5.4L 8, auto [CNG][17]	ULEV	11	14	$1,120	$140	18	2.85	**18**	▲
4.2L 6, auto	LEV	14	18	$1,410	$210	17	3.16	**15**	○
5.4L 8, auto	LEV	13	18	$1,500	$220	18	3.33	**14**	▽
4.2L 6, auto	Tier 1	14	18	$1,410	$250	17	3.42	**13**	▽

See pages 64-65 for explanation of data and symbols.
[12/13/14/15/16/17] *CNG fuel economy is given as gasoline-equivalent MPG.*

	Emission Standard	Fuel Economy City	Hwy	Fuel Cost/yr	Health Cost/yr	GHG tons/yr	EDX ¢/mi	Green Score	Class Ranking
LARGE VANS (cont.)									
GMC G1500/2500 SAVANA (CARGO)[18]									
4.3L 6, auto	LEV	15	18	$1,410	$190	16	2.96	**17**	○
5.0L 8, auto	Tier 1	15	19	$1,410	$210	16	3.10	**16**	○
4.3L 6, auto	Tier 1	15	18	$1,410	$220	16	3.11	**15**	○
5.7L 8, auto	LEV	14	17	$1,500	$210	17	3.20	**15**	○
5.7L 8, auto	Tier 1	14	17	$1,500	$250	17	3.45	**13**	✖
GMC G1500/2500 SAVANA (PASSENGER)[19]									
4.3L 6, auto	LEV	14	18	$1,410	$200	17	3.08	**16**	○
5.7L 8, auto	LEV	13	17	$1,500	$220	18	3.30	**14**	▽
5.0L 8, auto	Tier 1	14	18	$1,410	$250	17	3.39	**13**	▽
4.3L 6, auto	Tier 1	14	18	$1,410	$250	17	3.44	**13**	▽
5.7L 8, auto	Tier 1	13	17	$1,500	$260	18	3.56	**12**	✖
VOLKSWAGEN EUROVAN									
2.8L 6, auto	TLEV	17	20	$1,250	$200	15	2.86	**18**	▲
VOLKSWAGEN EUROVAN CAMPER									
2.8L 6, auto	TLEV	15	20	$1,320	$220	16	3.06	**16**	○

COMPACT PICKUPS

	Emission Standard	Fuel Economy City	Hwy	Fuel Cost/yr	Health Cost/yr	GHG tons/yr	EDX ¢/mi	Green Score	Class Ranking
CHEVROLET S-10[20]									
2.2L 4, manual	LEV	22	28	$940	$130	11	2.00	**28**	▲
2.2L 4, auto	LEV	19	25	$1,070	$140	12	2.20	**25**	▲
4.3L 6, auto	LEV	17	22	$1,180	$150	13	2.37	**23**	○
4.3L 6, manual	LEV	16	22	$1,250	$150	14	2.46	**22**	○
4.3L 6, auto 4wd	LEV	15	20	$1,320	$180	15	2.79	**18**	▽
4.3L 6, manual 4wd	LEV	14	17	$1,500	$190	17	3.03	**16**	✖
DODGE DAKOTA									
3.9L 6, auto	LEV	18	19	$1,250	$170	14	2.57	**21**	○
4.7L 8, auto	LEV	15	20	$1,410	$180	15	2.79	**18**	▽
3.9L 6, auto	Tier 1	18	19	$1,250	$200	14	2.80	**18**	▽
3.9L 6, auto 4wd	LEV	14	17	$1,410	$180	16	2.91	**17**	▽
4.7L 8, manual 4wd	LEV	14	18	$1,410	$190	16	2.94	**17**	▽
4.7L 8, auto	Tier 1	15	20	$1,410	$210	16	3.02	**16**	✖
4.7L 8, auto 4wd	LEV	13	18	$1,500	$190	17	3.06	**16**	✖
5.9L 8, auto	LEV	13	16	$1,610	$190	18	3.14	**15**	✖

See pages 64-65 for explanation of data and symbols.
[18/19] *A compressed natural gas (CNG)-gasoline bi-fuel version of this vehicle is also available.*
[20] *An ethanol-gasoline flex-fuel version of this vehicle is also available.*

	Emission Standard	Fuel Economy City	Hwy	Fuel Cost/yr	Health Cost/yr	GHG tons/yr	EDX ¢/mi	Green Score	Class Ranking
COMPACT PICKUPS (cont.)									
DODGE DAKOTA (cont.)									
4.7L 8, manual 4wd	Tier 1	14	18	$1,410	$220	17	3.17	**15**	✖
3.9L 6, auto 4wd	Tier 1	14	17	$1,410	$220	17	3.19	**15**	✖
4.7L 8, auto 4wd	Tier 1	13	18	$1,500	$220	17	3.30	**14**	✖
5.9L 8, auto	Tier 1	13	16	$1,610	$220	18	3.37	**14**	✖
5.9L 8, auto 4wd	Tier 1	12	16	$1,730	$230	19	3.52	**13**	✖
FORD EXPLORER SPORT TRAC[21]									
4.0L 6, manual	LEV	17	21	$1,250	$170	14	2.63	**20**	○
4.0L 6, auto	LEV	16	21	$1,250	$180	15	2.72	**19**	○
4.0L 6, manual 4wd	LEV	16	20	$1,320	$180	15	2.73	**19**	○
4.0L 6, auto 4wd	LEV	15	20	$1,320	$180	15	2.81	**18**	▽
FORD RANGER[22]									
Electric[23]	ZEV	2.9	2.9	$510	$130	8	1.68	**34**	✔
2.3L 4, manual	LEV	24	28	$900	$130	11	1.94	**29**	✔
2.3L 4, auto	LEV	21	25	$1,020	$140	12	2.12	**26**	▲
3.0L 6, manual	LEV	19	22	$1,130	$140	13	2.27	**24**	○
3.0L 6, auto	LEV	17	22	$1,180	$150	13	2.39	**23**	○
4.0L 6, auto	LEV	17	21	$1,250	$150	14	2.43	**22**	○
3.0L 6, manual 4wd	LEV	18	21	$1,180	$170	14	2.50	**21**	○
4.0L 6, manual	LEV	17	22	$1,180	$170	14	2.51	**21**	○
3.0L 6, auto 4wd	LEV	16	19	$1,320	$170	15	2.71	**19**	○
4.0L 6, manual 4wd	LEV	16	19	$1,320	$180	15	2.73	**19**	○
4.0L 6, auto 4wd	LEV	15	18	$1,410	$180	16	2.83	**18**	▽
GMC SONOMA[24]									
2.2L 4, manual	LEV	22	28	$940	$130	11	2.00	**28**	▲
2.2L 4, auto	LEV	19	25	$1,070	$140	12	2.20	**25**	▲
4.3L 6, auto	LEV	17	22	$1,180	$150	13	2.37	**23**	○
4.3L 6, manual	LEV	16	22	$1,250	$150	14	2.48	**22**	○
4.3L 6, auto 4wd	LEV	15	20	$1,320	$180	15	2.79	**18**	▽
4.3L 6, manual 4wd	LEV	14	17	$1,500	$190	17	3.03	**16**	✖
ISUZU HOMBRE									
2.2L 4, manual	LEV	22	28	$940	$130	11	2.00	**28**	▲
2.2L 4, auto	LEV	19	25	$1,070	$140	12	2.20	**25**	▲
MAZDA B2300									
2.3L 4, manual	LEV	24	28	$900	$130	11	1.94	**29**	✔
2.3L 4, auto	LEV	21	25	$1,020	$140	12	2.12	**26**	▲

See pages 64-65 for explanation of data and symbols.
[21]/[22]/[24] *An ethanol-gasoline flex-fuel version of this vehicle is also available.*
[23] *Electric vehicle fuel economy is given in mi/kWh.*

	Emission Standard	Fuel Economy City Hwy		Fuel Cost/yr	Health Cost/yr	GHG tons/yr	EDX ¢/mi	Green Score	Class Ranking

COMPACT PICKUPS (cont.)

MAZDA B3000[25]

3.0L 6, manual	LEV	19	22	$1,130	$140	13	2.27	**24**	○
3.0L 6, auto	LEV	17	22	$1,180	$150	13	2.39	**23**	○
3.0L 6, manual 4wd	LEV	18	21	$1,180	$160	13	2.45	**22**	○
3.0L 6, auto 4wd	LEV	16	19	$1,320	$170	15	2.71	**19**	○

MAZDA B4000

4.0L 6, manual	LEV	17	22	$1,180	$160	13	2.46	**22**	○
4.0L 6, auto	LEV	17	21	$1,250	$170	14	2.58	**21**	○
4.0L 6, manual 4wd	LEV	16	19	$1,320	$180	15	2.73	**19**	○
4.0L 6, auto 4wd	LEV	15	18	$1,410	$180	16	2.83	**18**	▽

NISSAN FRONTIER

2.4L 4, manual	LEV	22	25	$940	$130	11	2.04	**28**	▲
2.4L 4, auto	LEV	20	23	$1,070	$140	12	2.19	**25**	▲
3.3L 6, auto	LEV	16	20	$1,320	$170	15	2.67	**20**	○
3.3L 6, manual	LEV	16	19	$1,320	$170	15	2.68	**19**	○
3.3L 6, manual 4wd	LEV	16	18	$1,320	$170	15	2.69	**19**	○
3.3L 6, auto 4wd	LEV	15	19	$1,320	$180	15	2.73	**19**	○
3.3L 6, auto [P]	LEV	15	18	$1,460	$180	15	2.76	**19**	○
3.3L 6, manual [P]	LEV	15	18	$1,550	$180	15	2.80	**18**	▽
3.3L 6, manual 4wd [P]	LEV	15	18	$1,550	$180	16	2.86	**18**	▽
3.3L 6, auto 4wd [P]	LEV	15	18	$1,550	$180	16	2.86	**18**	▽

TOYOTA TACOMA

2.4L 4, manual	LEV	22	27	$940	$130	11	1.95	**29**	✔
2.4L 4, auto	LEV	22	25	$980	$130	11	2.02	**28**	▲
2.7L 4, auto	LEV	19	22	$1,130	$140	13	2.28	**24**	○
3.4L 6, manual	LEV	18	22	$1,130	$140	13	2.28	**24**	○
2.7L 4, auto 4wd	LEV	18	21	$1,180	$160	13	2.48	**22**	○
2.7L 4, manual 4wd	LEV	18	21	$1,180	$160	13	2.49	**22**	○
3.4L 6, auto	LEV	17	19	$1,250	$170	14	2.62	**20**	○
3.4L 6, manual 4wd	LEV	17	19	$1,250	$170	14	2.63	**20**	○
3.4L 6, auto 4wd	LEV	17	19	$1,320	$170	15	2.67	**20**	○

See pages 64-65 for explanation of data and symbols.
[25] *An ethanol-gasoline flex-fuel version of this vehicle is also available.*

	Emission Standard	Fuel Economy City Hwy		Fuel Cost/yr	Health Cost/yr	GHG tons/yr	EDX ¢/mi	Green Score	Class Ranking

STANDARD PICKUPS

CHEVROLET AVALANCHE

5.3L 8, auto	ULEV	14	18	$1,410	$210	17	3.18	15	○
5.3L 8, auto 4wd	ULEV	13	17	$1,610	$220	18	3.35	14	▽
5.3L 8, auto	Tier 1	14	18	$1,410	$260	17	3.49	13	▽
5.3L 8, auto 4wd	Tier 1	13	17	$1,610	$260	18	3.66	12	✖

CHEVROLET SILVERADO C1500[26]

4.8L 8, auto	LEV	15	20	$1,320	$180	15	2.80	18	▲
4.3L 6, manual	Tier 1	16	21	$1,250	$200	14	2.83	18	▲
5.3L 8, auto	ULEV	15	19	$1,410	$180	16	2.83	18	▲
4.8L 8, manual	Tier 1	16	20	$1,250	$200	15	2.87	18	○
4.3L 6, auto	Tier 1	15	20	$1,320	$200	15	2.94	17	○
4.8L 8, auto	Tier 1	15	20	$1,320	$210	15	2.95	17	○
5.3L 8, auto	Tier 1	15	19	$1,410	$210	16	3.06	16	○

CHEVROLET SILVERADO K1500[27]

5.3L 8, auto 4wd	ULEV	14	17	$1,500	$190	17	3.01	16	○
4.8L 8, auto 4wd	LEV	14	18	$1,410	$200	17	3.02	16	○
4.3L 6, auto 4wd	Tier 1	15	18	$1,410	$210	16	3.10	16	○
4.8L 8, manual 4wd	LEV	14	17	$1,500	$200	17	3.13	15	○
4.3L 6, manual 4wd	Tier 1	14	18	$1,500	$220	17	3.16	15	○
4.8L 8, auto 4wd	Tier 1	14	18	$1,410	$220	17	3.18	15	○
5.3L 8, auto 4wd	Tier 1	14	17	$1,500	$220	17	3.24	15	▽
4.8L 8, manual 4wd	Tier 1	14	17	$1,500	$220	17	3.28	14	▽

CHEVROLET SILVERADO K2500

6.0L 8, auto 4wd	HDT-LEV	12	15	$1,540	$240	20	3.63	12	✖
6.0L 8, auto 4wd	HDT	12	15	$1,540	$280	20	3.90	10	✖

DODGE RAM PICKUP 1500

4.7L 8, auto	ULEV	14	19	$1,410	$180	16	2.91	17	○
3.7L 6, auto	Tier 1	15	19	$1,320	$210	16	3.01	16	○
4.7L 8, manual 4wd	ULEV	14	17	$1,500	$190	17	3.04	16	○
4.7L 8, auto	Tier 1	14	19	$1,410	$220	16	3.13	15	○
4.7L 8, auto 4wd	ULEV	13	17	$1,610	$200	18	3.17	15	○
4.7L 8, manual 4wd	Tier 1	14	17	$1,500	$220	17	3.26	14	▽
5.9L 8, auto	ULEV	12	17	$1,610	$200	19	3.27	14	▽
4.7L 8, auto 4wd	Tier 1	13	17	$1,610	$230	18	3.39	13	▽
5.9L 8, auto 4wd	ULEV	11	15	$1,730	$210	20	3.41	13	▽
5.9L 8, auto	Tier 1	12	17	$1,610	$230	19	3.50	13	▽
5.9L 8, auto 4wd	Tier 1	11	15	$1,730	$240	20	3.64	12	✖

See pages 64-65 for explanation of data and symbols.
[26/27] *An ethanol-gasoline flex-fuel version of this vehicle is also available.*

	Emission Standard	Fuel Economy City Hwy		Fuel Cost/yr	Health Cost/yr	GHG tons/yr	EDX ¢/mi	Green Score	Class Ranking

STANDARD PICKUPS (cont.)

DODGE RAM PICKUP 2500

	Emission Standard	City	Hwy	Fuel Cost/yr	Health Cost/yr	GHG tons/yr	EDX ¢/mi	Green Score	Class Ranking
5.9L 8, auto	HDT-ULEV	11	17	$1,530	$230	19	3.52	13	✖
5.9L 8, auto 4wd	HDT-ULEV	11	15	$1,630	$240	20	3.72	11	✖
5.9L 8, auto	HDT	11	17	$1,530	$280	19	3.85	11	✖
5.9L 8, auto 4wd	HDT	11	15	$1,630	$290	21	4.05	10	✖

FORD F-150[28]

	Emission Standard	City	Hwy	Fuel Cost/yr	Health Cost/yr	GHG tons/yr	EDX ¢/mi	Green Score	Class Ranking
5.4L 8, auto [CNG][29]	SULEV	12	16	$1,620	$100	16	2.36	23	✔
4.2L 6, manual	ULEV	17	21	$1,250	$160	14	2.53	21	▲
5.4L 8, auto [CNG][30]	ULEV	12	16	$1,620	$130	17	2.59	20	▲
4.2L 6, auto	ULEV	16	20	$1,250	$170	15	2.67	20	▲
4.2L 6, manual 4wd	ULEV	16	19	$1,320	$170	15	2.74	19	▲
4.2L 6, auto 4wd	ULEV	15	19	$1,320	$180	15	2.75	19	▲
4.6L 8, auto	LEV	16	20	$1,320	$180	15	2.76	19	▲
4.6L 8, manual	LEV	15	19	$1,320	$190	16	2.85	18	○
5.4L 8, auto	LEV	15	19	$1,410	$190	16	2.87	18	○
4.6L 8, auto 4wd	LEV	14	18	$1,410	$200	17	3.02	16	○
4.6L 8, manual 4wd	LEV	14	18	$1,500	$200	17	3.05	16	○
5.4L 8, auto 4wd	LEV	14	17	$1,500	$200	17	3.09	16	○
5.4L 8, auto [P]	LEV	12	16	$1,900	$210	19	3.35	14	▽

FORD F-250 SUPER DUTY

	Emission Standard	City	Hwy	Fuel Cost/yr	Health Cost/yr	GHG tons/yr	EDX ¢/mi	Green Score	Class Ranking
5.4L 8, auto	HDT-LEV	14	18	$1,290	$220	17	3.19	15	▽
5.4L 8, auto 4wd	HDT-LEV	13	17	$1,420	$230	18	3.45	13	▽

GMC SIERRA C1500[31]

	Emission Standard	City	Hwy	Fuel Cost/yr	Health Cost/yr	GHG tons/yr	EDX ¢/mi	Green Score	Class Ranking
4.8L 8, manual	LEV	16	20	$1,250	$180	15	2.72	19	▲
4.8L 8, auto	LEV	15	20	$1,320	$180	15	2.80	18	▲
4.3L 6, manual	Tier 1	16	21	$1,250	$200	14	2.83	18	▲
5.3L 8, auto	ULEV	15	19	$1,410	$180	16	2.83	18	▲
4.8L 8, manual	Tier 1	16	20	$1,250	$200	15	2.87	18	○
4.3L 6, auto	Tier 1	15	20	$1,320	$200	15	2.94	17	○
4.8L 8, auto	Tier 1	15	20	$1,320	$210	15	2.95	17	○
5.3L 8, auto	Tier 1	15	19	$1,410	$210	16	3.06	16	○

GMC SIERRA DENALI

	Emission Standard	City	Hwy	Fuel Cost/yr	Health Cost/yr	GHG tons/yr	EDX ¢/mi	Green Score	Class Ranking
6.0L 8, auto Awd	LEV	12	15	$1,610	$230	19	3.51	13	✖
6.0L 8, auto Awd	Tier 1	12	15	$1,610	$270	19	3.76	11	✖

See pages 64-65 for explanation of data and symbols.
[28] *A compressed natural gas (CNG)-gasoline bi-fuel version of this vehicle is also available.*
[29/30] *CNG fuel economy is given as gasoline-equivalent MPG.*
[31] *An ethanol-gasoline flex-fuel version of this vehicle is also available.*

	Emission Standard	Fuel Economy City	Hwy	Fuel Cost/yr	Health Cost/yr	GHG tons/yr	EDX ¢/mi	Green Score	Class Ranking

STANDARD PICKUPS (cont.)

GMC SIERRA K1500[32]

5.3L 8, auto 4wd	ULEV	14	17	$1,500	$190	17	3.01	16	○
4.8L 8, auto 4wd	LEV	14	17	$1,410	$200	17	3.03	16	○
4.3L 6, auto 4wd	Tier 1	15	18	$1,410	$210	16	3.10	16	○
4.3L 6, manual 4wd	Tier 1	14	17	$1,500	$220	17	3.19	15	○
4.8L 8, auto 4wd	Tier 1	14	17	$1,410	$220	17	3.19	15	○
5.3L 8, auto 4wd	Tier 1	14	17	$1,500	$220	17	3.24	15	▽
4.8L 8, manual 4wd	Tier 1	14	17	$1,500	$220	17	3.28	14	▽

GMC SIERRA K2500

6.0L 8, auto 4wd	HDT-LEV	12	15	$1,540	$240	20	3.64	12	✖
6.0L 8, auto 4wd	HDT	12	15	$1,540	$280	20	3.91	10	✖

LINCOLN BLACKWOOD

5.4L 8, auto [P]	LEV	12	17	$1,770	$230	19	3.52	13	✖

TOYOTA TUNDRA

3.4L 6, manual	LEV	16	19	$1,250	$170	15	2.66	20	▲
3.4L 6, auto	LEV	16	19	$1,320	$170	15	2.67	20	▲
3.4L 6, manual 4wd	LEV	15	18	$1,410	$180	16	2.85	18	○
3.4L 6, auto 4wd	LEV	15	18	$1,410	$180	16	2.88	17	○
4.7L 8, auto	LEV	15	18	$1,410	$190	16	2.91	17	○
4.7L 8, auto 4wd	LEV	14	17	$1,500	$190	17	3.01	16	○
4.7L 8, auto	Tier 1	15	18	$1,410	$210	16	3.07	16	○
4.7L 8, auto 4wd	Tier 1	14	17	$1,500	$220	17	3.17	15	○

COMPACT SUVs

CHEVROLET TRACKER CONVERTIBLE

2.0L 4, auto	LEV	23	26	$940	$130	11	1.94	29	▲
2.0L 4, manual	LEV	23	26	$940	$130	11	1.94	29	▲
2.0L 4, manual 4wd	LEV	23	25	$940	$130	11	1.97	29	▲
2.0L 4, auto 4wd	LEV	22	25	$980	$130	11	1.98	29	○

CHEVROLET TRACKER HARDTOP

2.0L 4, auto	LEV	23	26	$940	$130	11	1.94	29	▲
2.0L 4, manual	LEV	23	26	$940	$130	11	1.94	29	▲
2.0L 4, manual 4wd	LEV	22	25	$980	$130	11	1.99	29	○
2.0L 4, auto 4wd	LEV	22	25	$980	$130	11	2.04	28	○

See pages 64-65 for explanation of data and symbols.
[32] *An ethanol-gasoline flex-fuel version of this vehicle is also available.*

	Emission Standard	Fuel Economy City Hwy	Fuel Cost/yr	Health Cost/yr	GHG tons/yr	EDX ¢/mi	Green Score	Class Ranking

COMPACT SUVs (cont.)

CHEVROLET TRACKER LT

2.5L 6, auto	LEV	19	21	$1,130	$150	13	2.31	**24**	▽
2.5L 6, auto 4wd	LEV	18	20	$1,180	$150	13	2.37	**23**	▽

CHEVROLET TRACKER ZR2

2.5L 6, auto	LEV	18	20	$1,180	$150	13	2.36	**23**	▽

CHEVROLET TRACKER ZR2 CONVERTIBLE

2.0L 4, manual 4wd	LEV	23	25	$940	$130	11	1.96	**29**	▲
2.0L 4, auto 4wd	LEV	22	25	$980	$130	11	2.00	**28**	○

FORD ESCAPE

2.0L 4, manual	LEV	23	27	$900	$130	11	1.97	**29**	▲
2.0L 4, manual 4wd	LEV	22	25	$980	$130	11	2.06	**27**	○
3.0L 6, auto	LEV	19	24	$1,070	$140	12	2.22	**25**	○
3.0L 6, auto 4wd	LEV	18	23	$1,130	$140	13	2.28	**24**	○

HONDA CR-V

2.4L 4, auto	LEV	23	28	$900	$130	11	1.97	**29**	▲
2.4L 4, auto 4wd	LEV	22	26	$940	$130	11	2.02	**28**	○
2.4L 4, manual 4wd	LEV	21	25	$980	$130	11	2.08	**27**	○

HYUNDAI SANTA FE

2.4L 4, manual	LEV	21	28	$940	$150	11	2.19	**26**	○
2.4L 4, auto	LEV	20	27	$980	$150	12	2.26	**25**	○
2.7L 6, auto	LEV	19	26	$1,020	$160	12	2.31	**24**	▽
2.7L 6, auto	LEV	19	23	$1,130	$160	13	2.40	**23**	▽

ISUZU RODEO SPORT

2.2L 4, manual	LEV	19	23	$1,130	$160	13	2.40	**23**	▽
2.2L 4, auto	LEV	17	22	$1,180	$170	14	2.53	**21**	✖
3.2L 6, manual 4wd	LEV	17	20	$1,250	$170	14	2.60	**20**	✖
3.2L 6, auto	LEV	16	20	$1,250	$170	14	2.63	**20**	✖
3.2L 6, auto 4wd	LEV	16	20	$1,250	$170	14	2.63	**20**	✖

JEEP LIBERTY

3.7L 6, auto	LEV	16	20	$1,250	$170	14	2.63	**20**	✖
3.7L 6, auto 4wd	LEV	16	20	$1,320	$180	15	2.73	**19**	✖

JEEP WRANGLER

2.5L 4, manual 4wd	TLEV	18	20	$1,180	$160	13	2.47	**22**	▽
2.5L 4, auto 4wd	TLEV	16	18	$1,320	$170	15	2.67	**20**	✖
4.0L 6, manual 4wd	LEV	15	18	$1,410	$180	16	2.80	**18**	✖
4.0L 6, auto 4wd	LEV	15	17	$1,410	$180	16	2.86	**18**	✖

See pages 64-65 for explanation of data and symbols.

	Emission Standard	Fuel Economy City Hwy		Fuel Cost/yr	Health Cost/yr	GHG tons/yr	EDX ¢/mi	Green Score	Class Ranking

COMPACT SUVs (cont.)

KIA SPORTAGE
2.0L 4, manual	LEV	19	23	$1,070	$140	12	2.22	**25**	○
2.0L 4, manual 4wd	LEV	19	22	$1,070	$140	12	2.23	**25**	○
2.0L 4, auto 4wd	LEV	18	21	$1,130	$150	13	2.32	**24**	▽
2.0L 4, auto	LEV	18	21	$1,180	$150	13	2.33	**24**	▽

LAND ROVER FREELANDER
2.5L 6, auto 4wd [P]	LEV	17	21	$1,380	$170	14	2.57	**21**	✖

LEXUS RX 300
3.0L 6, auto	LEV	19	23	$1,130	$150	13	2.28	**24**	○
3.0L 6, auto 4wd	LEV	18	22	$1,130	$150	13	2.33	**24**	▽

MAZDA TRIBUTE
2.0L 4, manual	LEV	23	27	$900	$130	11	1.97	**29**	▲
2.0L 4, manual 4wd	LEV	22	25	$980	$130	11	2.06	**27**	○
3.0L 6, auto	LEV	19	24	$1,070	$140	12	2.22	**25**	○
3.0L 6, auto 4wd	LEV	18	23	$1,130	$140	13	2.28	**24**	○

SATURN VUE
2.2L 4, auto CVT	ULEV	22	28	$940	$120	11	1.95	**29**	▲
2.2L 4, manual	LEV	23	28	$900	$130	11	1.96	**29**	▲
2.2L 4, auto CVT Awd	ULEV	21	26	$980	$130	11	2.02	**28**	○
3.0L 6, auto Awd	LEV	19	25	$1,070	$160	13	2.35	**23**	▽

SUBARU FORESTER
2.5L 4, auto Awd	LEV	22	27	$940	$130	11	1.99	**29**	○
2.5L 4, manual Awd	LEV	21	27	$980	$130	11	2.03	**28**	○

SUZUKI GRAND VITARA
2.5L 6, manual	LEV	19	22	$1,130	$140	13	2.25	**25**	○
2.5L 6, manual 4wd	LEV	19	21	$1,130	$140	13	2.29	**24**	○
2.5L 6, auto	LEV	19	21	$1,130	$140	13	2.30	**24**	▽
2.5L 6, auto 4wd	LEV	18	20	$1,180	$150	13	2.35	**23**	▽

SUZUKI GRAND VITARA XL-7
2.7L 6, manual	LEV	18	20	$1,180	$170	14	2.54	**21**	✖
2.7L 6, manual 4wd	LEV	17	20	$1,180	$170	14	2.55	**21**	✖
2.7L 6, auto	LEV	17	20	$1,250	$170	14	2.58	**20**	✖
2.7L 6, auto 4wd	LEV	17	20	$1,250	$170	14	2.60	**20**	✖

See pages 64-65 for explanation of data and symbols.

	Emission Standard	Fuel Economy City	Fuel Economy Hwy	Fuel Cost/yr	Health Cost/yr	GHG tons/yr	EDX ¢/mi	Green Score	Class Ranking
COMPACT SUVs (cont.)									
SUZUKI VITARA 2-DOOR									
2.0L 4, manual	LEV	23	26	$940	$130	11	1.94	29	▲
2.0L 4, auto	LEV	22	25	$980	$130	11	1.98	29	○
2.0L 4, manual 4wd	LEV	22	25	$980	$130	11	1.99	29	○
2.0L 4, auto 4wd	LEV	22	25	$980	$130	11	1.99	28	○
SUZUKI VITARA 4-DOOR									
2.0L 4, manual	LEV	22	25	$980	$130	11	1.99	29	○
2.0L 4, manual 4wd	LEV	22	25	$980	$130	11	1.99	29	○
2.0L 4, auto	LEV	22	25	$980	$130	11	1.99	28	○
2.0L 4, auto 4wd	LEV	22	25	$980	$130	11	2.04	28	○
TOYOTA RAV4									
Electric[33]	ZEV	3.7	2.9	$450	$70	5	0.99	52	✔
2.0L 4, manual	LEV	25	31	$830	$120	10	1.80	32	✔
2.0L 4, auto	LEV	24	29	$870	$120	10	1.86	31	✔
2.0L 4, auto 4wd	LEV	23	27	$900	$130	11	1.98	29	○
2.0L 4, manual 4wd	LEV	22	27	$940	$130	11	2.00	28	○
MIDSIZE SUVs									
ACURA MDX									
3.5L 6, auto 4wd [P]	ULEV	17	23	$1,300	$160	14	2.48	22	▲
BMW X5 3.0i									
3.0L 6, manual 4wd [P]	ULEV	15	21	$1,460	$180	15	2.75	19	○
3.0L 6, auto stk 4wd [P]	ULEV	15	21	$1,460	$180	15	2.76	19	○
3.0L 6, manual 4wd [P]	Tier 1	15	21	$1,460	$210	15	2.97	17	▽
3.0L 6, auto stk 4wd [P]	Tier 1	15	21	$1,460	$210	15	2.98	17	▽
BMW X5 4.4i									
4.4L 8, auto 4wd [P]	LEV	13	17	$1,650	$200	17	3.13	15	✖
4.4L 8, auto 4wd [P]	Tier 1	13	17	$1,650	$220	17	3.28	14	✖
BMW X5 4.6is									
4.6L 8, auto stk 4wd [P]	LEV	12	17	$1,770	$210	18	3.27	14	✖
4.6L 8, auto stk 4wd [P]	Tier 1	12	17	$1,770	$230	18	3.43	13	✖

See pages 64-65 for explanation of data and symbols.
[33] Electric vehicle fuel economy is given in mi/kWh.

	Emission Standard	Fuel Economy City Hwy	Fuel Cost/yr	Health Cost/yr	GHG tons/yr	EDX ¢/mi	Green Score	Class Ranking
MIDSIZE SUVs (cont.)								
BUICK RENDEZVOUS								
3.4L 6, auto	ULEV	19 26	$1,020	$150	12	2.24	**25**	✔
3.4L 6, auto	LEV	19 26	$1,020	$160	12	2.31	**24**	✔
3.4L 6, auto Awd	ULEV	18 24	$1,130	$160	13	2.41	**22**	▲
3.4L 6, auto Awd	LEV	18 24	$1,130	$170	13	2.48	**22**	▲
CHEVROLET BLAZER								
4.3L 6, auto	LEV	17 22	$1,180	$170	14	2.52	**21**	▲
4.3L 6, manual	LEV	16 22	$1,250	$170	14	2.64	**20**	○
4.3L 6, auto 4wd	LEV	15 20	$1,320	$180	15	2.79	**18**	○
4.3L 6, manual 4wd	LEV	14 17	$1,500	$190	17	3.03	**16**	▽
CHEVROLET TRAILBLAZER								
4.2L 6, auto	LEV	16 22	$1,250	$180	15	2.69	**19**	○
4.2L 6, auto 4wd	LEV	15 21	$1,250	$180	15	2.72	**19**	○
DODGE DURANGO								
4.7L 8, auto	ULEV	15 20	$1,410	$180	16	2.80	**18**	○
4.7L 8, auto	ULEV	14 19	$1,410	$180	16	2.88	**18**	▽
4.7L 8, auto	Tier 1	15 20	$1,410	$210	16	3.02	**16**	▽
4.7L 8, auto 4wd	ULEV	13 17	$1,500	$190	17	3.05	**16**	▽
4.7L 8, auto 4wd	ULEV	13 18	$1,500	$190	17	3.08	**16**	▽
4.7L 8, auto	Tier 1	14 19	$1,410	$210	16	3.10	**16**	▽
5.9L 8, auto	ULEV	12 17	$1,610	$200	18	3.21	**15**	✖
4.7L 8, auto 4wd	Tier 1	13 17	$1,500	$220	17	3.28	**14**	✖
5.9L 8, auto 4wd	ULEV	12 16	$1,730	$200	19	3.30	**14**	✖
4.7L 8, auto 4wd	Tier 1	13 18	$1,500	$220	17	3.30	**14**	✖
5.9L 8, auto	Tier 1	12 17	$1,610	$230	18	3.43	**13**	✖
5.9L 8, auto 4wd	Tier 1	12 16	$1,730	$230	19	3.52	**13**	✖
FORD EXPLORER[34]								
4.0L 6, manual	LEV	17 21	$1,250	$170	14	2.63	**20**	○
4.0L 6, auto	LEV	16 21	$1,250	$180	15	2.72	**19**	○
4.0L 6, manual 4wd	LEV	16 20	$1,320	$180	15	2.73	**19**	○
4.0L 6, auto 4wd	LEV	15 20	$1,320	$180	15	2.81	**18**	○
4.6L 8, auto	LEV	14 19	$1,410	$180	16	2.88	**17**	▽
4.6L 8, auto 4wd	LEV	14 19	$1,410	$190	16	2.93	**17**	▽

See pages 64-65 for explanation of data and symbols.
[34] *An ethanol-gasoline flex-fuel version of this vehicle is also available.*

	Emission Standard	Fuel Economy City	Hwy	Fuel Cost/yr	Health Cost/yr	GHG tons/yr	EDX ¢/mi	Green Score	Class Ranking

MIDSIZE SUVs (cont.)

FORD EXPLORER SPORT[35]

4.0L 6, manual	LEV	17	22	$1,180	$170	14	2.51	21	▲
4.0L 6, auto	LEV	17	21	$1,250	$170	14	2.58	21	○
4.0L 6, manual 4wd	LEV	16	19	$1,320	$180	15	2.73	19	○
4.0L 6, auto 4wd	LEV	15	20	$1,320	$180	15	2.81	18	○

GMC ENVOY

4.2L 6, auto	LEV	16	22	$1,250	$180	15	2.69	19	○
4.2L 6, auto 4wd	LEV	15	21	$1,320	$180	15	2.81	18	○

GMC JIMMY

4.3L 6, auto	LEV	17	22	$1,180	$170	14	2.52	21	▲
4.3L 6, manual	LEV	16	22	$1,250	$170	14	2.64	20	○
4.3L 6, auto 4wd	LEV	15	20	$1,320	$180	15	2.79	18	○
4.3L 6, manual 4wd	LEV	14	17	$1,500	$190	17	3.03	16	▽

HONDA PASSPORT

3.2L 6, manual	LEV	17	20	$1,250	$170	14	2.59	20	○
3.2L 6, auto	LEV	17	21	$1,180	$170	14	2.62	20	○
3.2L 6, manual 4wd	LEV	17	20	$1,250	$170	14	2.64	20	○
3.2L 6, auto 4wd	LEV	16	20	$1,250	$180	15	2.68	19	○

INFINITI QX4

3.5L 6, auto	LEV	15	19	$1,320	$180	15	2.79	18	○
3.5L 6, auto 4wd	LEV	15	18	$1,410	$180	16	2.86	18	▽

ISUZU AXIOM

3.5L 6, auto	LEV	16	20	$1,250	$170	14	2.64	20	○
3.5L 6, auto 4wd	LEV	16	20	$1,320	$180	15	2.75	19	○

ISUZU RODEO

2.2L 4, manual	LEV	19	23	$1,130	$160	13	2.40	23	▲
2.2L 4, auto	LEV	17	22	$1,180	$170	14	2.51	21	▲
3.2L 6, manual	LEV	17	20	$1,250	$170	14	2.59	20	○
3.2L 6, auto	LEV	17	21	$1,180	$170	14	2.62	20	○
3.2L 6, manual 4wd	LEV	17	20	$1,250	$170	14	2.64	20	○
3.2L 6, auto 4wd	LEV	16	20	$1,250	$180	15	2.68	19	○

ISUZU TROOPER

3.5L 6, manual 4wd	LEV	16	19	$1,320	$180	15	2.80	18	○
3.5L 6, auto	LEV	15	19	$1,320	$180	15	2.80	18	○
3.5L 6, auto 4wd	LEV	15	19	$1,320	$180	16	2.82	18	○

See pages 64-65 for explanation of data and symbols.
[35] An ethanol-gasoline flex-fuel version of this vehicle is also available.

	Emission Standard	Fuel Economy City Hwy	Fuel Cost/yr	Health Cost/yr	GHG tons/yr	EDX ¢/mi	Green Score	Class Ranking

MIDSIZE SUVs (cont.)

JEEP GRAND CHEROKEE

4.0L 6, auto	LEV	15 21	$1,320	$170	15	2.69	**19**	○
4.0L 6, auto 4wd	LEV	15 20	$1,320	$180	15	2.76	**19**	○
4.7L 8, auto	LEV	14 19	$1,410	$180	16	2.85	**18**	▽
4.7L 8, auto 4wd	LEV	14 19	$1,500	$190	17	2.98	**17**	▽

LAND ROVER DISCOVERY SERIES II

4.0L 8, auto 4wd [P]	LEV	13 17	$1,650	$200	18	3.16	**15**	✖
4.0L 8, auto 4wd [P]	Tier 1	13 17	$1,650	$220	18	3.32	**14**	✖

MERCEDES-BENZ G500

5.0L 8, auto stk 4wd [P]	LEV	12 14	$1,900	$240	20	3.61	**12**	✖
5.0L 8, auto stk 4wd [P]	Tier 1	12 14	$1,900	$270	20	3.87	**11**	✖

MERCEDES-BENZ ML320

3.2L 6, auto 4wd [P]	ULEV	15 19	$1,460	$180	16	2.81	**18**	○
3.2L 6, auto 4wd [P]	Tier 1	15 19	$1,460	$210	16	3.04	**16**	▽

MERCEDES-BENZ ML500

5.0L 8, auto 4wd [P]	LEV	14 17	$1,650	$200	17	3.08	**16**	▽
5.0L 8, auto 4wd [P]	Tier 1	14 17	$1,650	$220	17	3.23	**15**	✖

MERCEDES-BENZ ML55 AMG

5.5L 8, auto 4wd [P]	LEV	14 17	$1,650	$210	17	3.20	**15**	✖
5.5L 8, auto 4wd [P]	Tier 1	14 17	$1,650	$220	17	3.23	**15**	✖

MERCURY MOUNTAINEER

4.0L 6, auto	LEV	16 21	$1,250	$180	15	2.72	**19**	○
4.0L 6, auto 4wd	LEV	15 20	$1,320	$180	15	2.81	**18**	○
4.0L 6, auto 4wd	LEV	15 19	$1,410	$180	16	2.85	**18**	▽
4.6L 8, auto	LEV	14 19	$1,410	$180	16	2.88	**17**	▽
4.6L 8, auto 4wd	LEV	14 18	$1,500	$190	17	2.98	**17**	▽

MITSUBISHI MONTERO

3.5L 6, auto 4wd [P]	LEV	15 19	$1,460	$180	15	2.80	**18**	○
3.5L 6, auto stk 4wd [P]	LEV	14 19	$1,550	$190	16	2.97	**17**	▽

MITSUBISHI MONTERO SPORT

3.0L 6, auto	LEV	18 22	$1,130	$160	13	2.47	**22**	▲
3.0L 6, auto 4wd	LEV	17 20	$1,250	$170	14	2.64	**20**	○
3.5L 6, auto 4wd	LEV	16 18	$1,320	$180	15	2.81	**18**	○

See pages 64-65 for explanation of data and symbols.

	Emission Standard	Fuel Economy City	Hwy	Fuel Cost/yr	Health Cost/yr	GHG tons/yr	EDX ¢/mi	Green Score	Class Ranking

MIDSIZE SUVs (cont.)

NISSAN PATHFINDER

3.5L 6, manual	LEV	17	19	$1,250	$170	14	2.61	**20**	○
3.5L 6, auto	LEV	16	19	$1,320	$170	15	2.69	**19**	○
3.5L 6, manual 4wd	LEV	16	18	$1,320	$180	15	2.76	**19**	○
3.5L 6, auto 4wd	LEV	15	18	$1,410	$180	16	2.86	**18**	▽
3.3L 6, auto	Tier 1	16	19	$1,320	$200	15	2.91	**17**	▽

NISSAN XTERRA

2.4L 4, manual	LEV	19	24	$1,070	$160	13	2.38	**23**	▲
3.3L 6, auto	LEV	16	20	$1,250	$170	14	2.63	**20**	○
3.3L 6, manual	LEV	16	19	$1,320	$170	15	2.68	**19**	○
3.3L 6, auto [P]	LEV	15	19	$1,460	$180	15	2.73	**19**	○
3.3L 6, manual 4wd	LEV	16	18	$1,320	$180	15	2.74	**19**	○
3.3L 6, manual [P]	LEV	15	19	$1,460	$180	15	2.74	**19**	○
3.3L 6, auto 4wd	LEV	15	19	$1,320	$180	15	2.79	**18**	○
3.3L 6, manual 4wd [P]	LEV	15	18	$1,550	$180	16	2.86	**18**	▽
3.3L 6, auto 4wd [P]	LEV	15	18	$1,550	$180	16	2.86	**18**	▽

OLDSMOBILE BRAVADA

4.2L 6, auto	LEV	16	22	$1,250	$180	15	2.69	**19**	○
4.2L 6, auto Awd	LEV	15	21	$1,320	$180	15	2.81	**18**	○

PONTIAC AZTEK

3.4L 6, auto	ULEV	19	26	$1,020	$150	12	2.24	**25**	✔
3.4L 6, auto	LEV	19	26	$1,020	$160	12	2.31	**24**	✔
3.4L 6, auto Awd	ULEV	18	24	$1,130	$160	13	2.41	**22**	▲
3.4L 6, auto Awd	LEV	18	24	$1,130	$170	13	2.48	**22**	▲

TOYOTA 4RUNNER

3.4L 6, auto	LEV	17	19	$1,250	$170	14	2.62	**20**	○
3.4L 6, auto 4wd	LEV	16	19	$1,320	$170	15	2.67	**20**	○

TOYOTA HIGHLANDER

2.4L 4, auto	LEV	22	27	$940	$150	11	2.16	**26**	✔
2.4L 4, auto 4wd	LEV	19	24	$1,070	$160	13	2.35	**23**	✔
3.0L 6, auto	LEV	19	23	$1,130	$160	13	2.40	**23**	▲
3.0L 6, auto 4wd	LEV	18	22	$1,130	$160	13	2.46	**22**	▲

See pages 64-65 for explanation of data and symbols.

	Emission Standard	Fuel Economy City	Hwy	Fuel Cost/yr	Health Cost/yr	GHG tons/yr	EDX ¢/mi	Green Score	Class Ranking

LARGE SUVs

CADILLAC ESCALADE
5.3L 8, auto	ULEV	14	18	$1,410	$210	17	3.11	**15**	▲
5.3L 8, auto	Tier 1	14	18	$1,410	$250	17	3.42	**13**	○
6.0L 8, auto Awd	LEV	12	15	$1,730	$240	20	3.70	**12**	▽
6.0L 8, auto Awd	Tier 1	12	15	$1,730	$280	20	3.95	**10**	✖

CADILLAC ESCALADE EXT
6.0L 8, auto Awd	LEV	12	15	$1,730	$240	20	3.70	**12**	▽
6.0L 8, auto Awd	Tier 1	12	15	$1,730	$280	20	3.95	**10**	✖

CHEVROLET SUBURBAN C1500[36]
5.3L 8, auto	ULEV	14	18	$1,410	$210	17	3.11	**15**	▲
5.3L 8, auto	Tier 1	14	18	$1,410	$250	17	3.43	**13**	○

CHEVROLET SUBURBAN K1500[37]
5.3L 8, auto 4wd	ULEV	13	17	$1,610	$220	18	3.35	**14**	○
5.3L 8, auto 4wd	Tier 1	13	17	$1,500	$260	18	3.60	**12**	▽

CHEVROLET SUBURBAN K2500
6.0L 8, auto 4wd	HDT-LEV	11	15	$1,600	$250	20	3.76	**11**	▽
6.0L 8, auto 4wd	HDT	11	15	$1,600	$290	20	4.03	**10**	✖

CHEVROLET TAHOE C1500[38]
4.8L 8, auto	LEV	15	19	$1,410	$210	16	3.08	**16**	▲
5.3L 8, auto	ULEV	14	18	$1,410	$210	17	3.11	**15**	▲
4.8L 8, auto	Tier 1	15	19	$1,410	$250	16	3.34	**14**	○
5.3L 8, auto	Tier 1	14	18	$1,410	$250	17	3.42	**13**	○

CHEVROLET TAHOE K1500[39]
5.3L 8, auto 4wd	ULEV	14	17	$1,500	$210	17	3.19	**15**	▲
4.8L 8, auto 4wd	LEV	14	17	$1,500	$220	17	3.22	**15**	○
4.8L 8, auto 4wd	Tier 1	14	17	$1,500	$250	17	3.47	**13**	○
5.3L 8, auto 4wd	Tier 1	14	17	$1,500	$260	18	3.53	**12**	○

FORD EXCURSION
5.4L 8, auto	HDT-LEV	12	16	$1,530	$250	20	3.75	**11**	▽
5.4L 8, auto 4wd	HDT-LEV	11	15	$1,620	$260	21	3.95	**10**	✖

FORD EXPEDITION
4.6L 8, auto	LEV	15	20	$1,320	$200	15	2.94	**17**	▲
4.6L 8, auto 4wd	LEV	14	17	$1,500	$220	17	3.27	**14**	○
5.4L 8, auto	LEV	13	18	$1,500	$220	18	3.33	**14**	○
5.4L 8, auto 4wd	LEV	12	16	$1,610	$230	19	3.54	**12**	○

See pages 64-65 for explanation of data and symbols.
[36]/[37]/[38]/[39] *An ethanol-gasoline flex-fuel version of this vehicle is also available.*

	Emission Standard	Fuel Economy City	Hwy	Fuel Cost/yr	Health Cost/yr	GHG tons/yr	EDX ¢/mi	Green Score	Class Ranking
LARGE SUVs (cont.)									
GMC YUKON C1500[40]									
4.8L 8, auto	LEV	15	19	$1,410	$210	16	3.08	**16**	▲
5.3L 8, auto	ULEV	14	18	$1,410	$210	17	3.11	**15**	▲
4.8L 8, auto	Tier 1	15	19	$1,410	$250	16	3.34	**14**	○
5.3L 8, auto	Tier 1	14	18	$1,410	$250	17	3.42	**13**	○
GMC YUKON DENALI									
6.0L 8, auto Awd	LEV	12	15	$1,730	$240	20	3.70	**12**	▽
6.0L 8, auto Awd	Tier 1	12	15	$1,730	$280	20	3.95	**10**	✖
GMC YUKON K1500[41]									
4.8L 8, auto 4wd	LEV	14	17	$1,500	$220	17	3.22	**15**	○
5.3L 8, auto 4wd	ULEV	13	17	$1,500	$220	18	3.28	**14**	○
4.8L 8, auto 4wd	Tier 1	14	17	$1,500	$250	17	3.47	**13**	○
5.3L 8, auto 4wd	Tier 1	14	17	$1,500	$260	18	3.53	**12**	○
GMC YUKON XL C1500[42]									
5.3L 8, auto	ULEV	14	18	$1,410	$210	17	3.11	**15**	▲
5.3L 8, auto	Tier 1	14	18	$1,410	$250	17	3.43	**13**	○
GMC YUKON XL DENALI									
6.0L 8, auto Awd	LEV	12	15	$1,730	$240	20	3.70	**12**	▽
6.0L 8, auto Awd	Tier 1	12	15	$1,730	$280	20	3.95	**10**	✖
GMC YUKON XL K1500[43]									
5.3L 8, auto 4wd	ULEV	13	17	$1,610	$220	18	3.35	**14**	○
5.3L 8, auto 4wd	Tier 1	13	17	$1,500	$260	18	3.60	**12**	▽
GMC YUKON XL K2500									
6.0L 8, auto 4wd	HDT-LEV	12	15	$1,580	$250	20	3.74	**11**	▽
6.0L 8, auto 4wd	HDT	12	15	$1,580	$290	20	4.01	**10**	✖
LAND ROVER RANGE ROVER									
4.6L 8, auto 4wd [P]	LEV	12	15	$1,900	$210	19	3.42	**13**	○
4.6L 8, auto 4wd [P]	Tier 1	12	15	$1,900	$240	19	3.57	**12**	○
LEXUS LX 470									
4.7L 8, auto 4wd	LEV	13	16	$1,610	$230	19	3.47	**13**	○
4.7L 8, auto 4wd	Tier 1	13	16	$1,610	$270	19	3.73	**11**	▽
LINCOLN NAVIGATOR									
5.4L 8, auto [P]	LEV	12	17	$1,770	$230	19	3.52	**13**	○
5.4L 8, auto 4wd [P]	LEV	12	16	$1,900	$240	20	3.65	**12**	▽

See pages 64-65 for explanation of data and symbols.
[40]/[41]/[42]/[43] *An ethanol-gasoline flex-fuel version of this vehicle is also available.*

	Emission Standard	Fuel Economy City	Hwy	Fuel Cost/yr	Health Cost/yr	GHG tons/yr	EDX ¢/mi	Green Score	Class Ranking
LARGE SUVs (cont.)									
TOYOTA LAND CRUISER									
4.7L 8, auto 4wd	LEV	13	16	$1,610	$230	19	3.47	**13**	○
4.7L 8, auto 4wd	Tier 1	13	16	$1,610	$270	19	3.73	**11**	▽
TOYOTA SEQUOIA									
4.7L 8, auto	ULEV	14	18	$1,410	$210	17	3.12	**15**	▲
4.7L 8, auto 4wd	ULEV	14	17	$1,500	$210	17	3.19	**15**	▲
4.7L 8, auto	Tier 1	14	18	$1,410	$250	17	3.43	**13**	○
4.7L 8, auto 4wd	Tier 1	14	17	$1,500	$250	17	3.50	**13**	○

See pages 64-65 for explanation of data and symbols.

Driving Green

Buying green is just the first step in reducing the environmental impacts of automobile use. Your choice of vehicle is most important, but how you drive and how well you maintain your car, van, or light truck will also make a difference.

Drive Carefully and Gently

- Avoid "jack rabbit" starts and aggressive driving. Flooring the gas pedal not only wastes gas, it leads to drastically higher pollution rates. One second of high-powered driving can produce nearly the same volume of carbon monoxide emissions as a half hour of normal driving.

- Think ahead. Try to anticipate stops and let your vehicle coast down as much as possible. Avoid the increased pollution, wasted gas, and wear on your brakes created by accelerating hard and braking hard.

- Follow the speed limit! Driving 75 mph instead of 65 mph will lower your fuel economy by about 10 percent, and can dramatically increase tailpipe pollution in many vehicles.

- When possible, plan your trips to avoid rush hour. Stop-and-go driving burns gas and increases emissions of smog-forming pollutants.

- Combine trips. Warmed-up engines and catalysts generate much less air pollution, so combining several short trips into one can make a big difference.

- Take a load off. Carrying around an extra 100 pounds reduces fuel economy by about 1 percent. Take a few moments to unload your cargo area.

- If your vehicle has it, use overdrive gear at cruising speeds. When driving a manual transmission, shift up as soon as possible. Running in a higher gear decreases the rpm and will decrease fuel use and engine wear.

- Try using the vents and opening windows to cool off before you turn on the air conditioner. Air conditioner use increases fuel

> ## Whatever Vehicle You Use, It's Greener with Two Passengers in It Than It Is with One, and It's Greener Still with Three.
>
> *ACEEE's Green Book™* ratings are based on a given vehicle's environmental performance. But it's also fair to look at greenness in terms of how a vehicle is used. Pollution per person is lower when more than one passenger is carried. For example, if you regularly carry three in a car or van, you can think of your household's per-person pollution as being one-third lower than that of someone who mostly drives alone in the same model.

consumption, increases NO_x emissions in some vehicles, and involves environmentally damaging fluids.

- Unlike many older cars and trucks, modern vehicles don't need to warm up and they have automatic chokes, so you don't need to step on the gas pedal before starting the engine.

Maintenance Tips

Your owner's manual is the best source of information about how to care for your vehicle. Refer to it for instructions about proper maintenance and service specific to your make and model.

- Keep your tires properly inflated. Tires should be inflated to the pressure recommended for your vehicle; this information is often printed inside the door frame or in your owner's manual. For every 3 pounds below recommended pressure, fuel economy goes down by about 1 percent. Tires can lose about 1 pound of pressure in a month, so check the air pressure regularly and always before going on a long trip or carrying heavy loads. Underinflated tires can also detract from handling, safety, and how long the tires will last.

- Check your own fuel economy every few weeks. If you notice it slipping, that could mean you have a minor problem with the engine or your brakes. Using this advance warning, you can fix problems before you have a breakdown on the road.

- Get a tune-up. Whether you do it yourself or go to a mechanic, a tune-up can increase your fuel economy. Follow owner's manual guidelines. Be sure to check for worn spark plugs, dragging brakes,

---

Checking Your Gas Mileage

You can check your MPG for yourself with these three easy steps:

1. Fill the tank and jot down the odometer reading.

2. Next time you buy gas, fill the tank again and note the new odometer reading and the number of gallons you purchased.

3. Subtract the old odometer reading from the new one and divide this number by the number of gallons you bought.

The result is your miles per gallon (MPG).

---

and low transmission fluid, have your wheels aligned and tires rotated, and replace the air filter if needed. Make sure all used vehicle fluids are recycled or disposed of safely.

■ Change the oil. In addition to making your car or truck last longer, replacing the oil and oil filter regularly will also help fuel economy. Check your owner's manual for specific recommendations about how often to change. Ask the service station if they recycle used oil, or if you do it yourself, take your old oil to someplace that does recycle. Ask for recycled oil as a replacement.

■ Have your vehicle's emission control system checked periodically. Take it in for service if an instrument panel warning light comes on.

Careful Fill-Ups

Americans too often take gasoline for granted, forgetting that it is quite a hazardous substance. Gasoline fumes are toxic and carcinogenic; they cause smog; and spilled gasoline can pollute the water and poison wildlife. And it's very flammable, too.

■ Use regular gasoline unless your owner's manual says otherwise. Unless your car requires premium, high-octane fuels improve neither fuel economy nor performance and will just waste your money.

■ Don't overfill the gas tank or try to top it off beyond where the automatic nozzle clicks off. Spilled gasoline evaporates to aggravate smog formation and can leak into groundwater.

■ Patronize gas stations that have vapor-recovery nozzles (those black, accordion-looking plastic devices attached to the nozzle) whenever you can.

Green Buyer Alert
Cleaner Cars Need Cleaner Gasoline

Every time you fill up, a small amount of sulfur goes into your fuel tank, but it doesn't take much sulfur to greatly worsen the pollution coming from a car or truck. Sulfur is a chemical element present in crude oil that is not always removed when gasoline is refined. Burning sulfur-laden fuel produces sulfur dioxide (SO_2), which is both a direct pollutant and a source of fine particles that damage your lungs. Sulfur poisons a car's catalytic converter, diminishing its ability to remove other pollutants from the exhaust. Thus, the level of sulfur in gasoline, which varies throughout the country, can dramatically affect vehicle emissions

Some of the cleanest cars and trucks (such as Low-Emission Vehicles) are quite susceptible to sulfur poisoning. Getting the full benefits of a LEV or ULEV vehicle depends on having clean gasoline, ideally low-sulfur fuel as required in California. Some oil companies are beginning to market low-sulfur gasoline in other areas, so look for it when you fill up.

Prudent Parking

- Park in the shade in summer to keep your car cool and minimize evaporation of fuel.

- If you have a garage, use it as much as possible to keep your car warm in winter and cool in summer.

- If you have to park outdoors, windshield shades can cut down on summer heat and help keep the frost off in the winter.

Take Advantage of "Commuter Choice" Programs

Most Americans commute to work, and now there are special programs that provide incentives for both employees and employers to "Get There With Clean Air." The U.S. Environmental Protection Agency and U.S. Department of Transportation are teaming up with businesses and others to set up "Commuter Choice" programs. These employer-sponsored initiatives can make you eligible for cash and other benefits for greener commuting. Examples include:

- One company gives their workers free walking shoes, with the promotion "we'll even buy your walking shoes if you hoof it to work!"

- Another company offers participating employees monthly drawings for prizes that might include extra time off, mountain bikes, and other goodies.

- A municipality gives its employees an extra hour of time-off for every 5 days they use carpool or vanpool to get to work, plus permission to dress casually at the office.

Companies and communities that make use of Commuter Choice benefits often save money. For example, by cutting down on car commuting, they can avoid the need to build large parking lots that are both expensive and use up green space. These programs take advantage of recent fringe benefits rules, such as offering workers tax-free transit or vanpool benefits of up to $65 per month. Employers can also allow employees to "cash-out" their parking space, receiving additional income of up to $175 per month (taxed like added salary for the employee, but still a deductible business expense for the employer). Employees can use this cash to commute as they wish, including carpooling, telecommuting, bicycling, or walking. Employers benefit through lowered taxes, lowered costs, and new ways to recruit and keep employees.

Commuter Choice cuts pollution, reduces traffic congestion, and conserves energy. Ask your employer if they have a Commuter Choice program. If not, ask them to start one. For more information, see the Commuter Choice link under "Other Resources" on the GreenerCars.com Links page.

Automobiles and the Environment

Automobiles affect the environment in many ways. Impacts begin when a vehicle is manufactured (including the production of all the parts and materials that go into the car) and end with its scrappage in a junkyard (which can recycle many parts but also involves the disposal of many wastes). Over the life of an average motor vehicle, however, much of the environmental damage occurs during driving and is greatly associated with fuel consumption. The figure on the following page illustrates the breakdown of life-cycle ("cradle to grave") energy use for a typical automobile. Nearly 90 percent is due to fuel consumption over the dozen or so years of a vehicle's life.

Environmental impacts start with mineral extraction and the production of the raw materials that go into the parts of a car. For example, iron ore gets turned into steel, which now accounts for most of the mass in vehicles. Steel can be recycled, of course. On average, today's automobiles are about 75 percent recyclable, and using recycled steel helps reduce energy use and pollution. Other metal components, such as aluminum (used in some engine parts and wheels, for example) and copper (used for wiring) are also largely recycled. The lead and acid in batteries are poisonous and dangerous. But batteries can be recycled, if they are returned to a service station, a parts store, or brought to a municipal hazardous waste facility. Plastics, which are mostly made from petroleum, are more difficult to recycle. In any case, some degree of pollution is associated with all of these components, much of it due to the energy consumption, air pollution, and releases of toxic substances that occur when automobiles are manufactured and distributed.

Most of the environmental impact associated with motor vehicles occurs when they are used, due to pollution in their exhaust and pollution associated with supplying the fuel. In the United States, nearly all of today's automobiles use gasoline; a lesser number use diesel fuel. In some areas, various alternative fuels are being introduced, but these are not widely available for most drivers. When gasoline, diesel, or other fuels are burned in car engines, combustion is never perfect, and so a mix of hazardous pollutants comes out the tailpipe.

LIFECYCLE ENERGY USE FOR A TYPICAL AUTOMOBILE

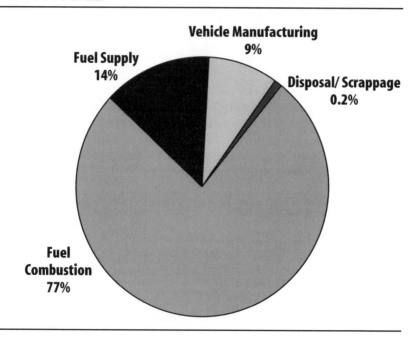

Vehicle Manufacturing 9%

Fuel Supply 14%

Disposal/ Scrappage 0.2%

Fuel Combustion 77%

If combustion were perfect and didn't create noxious by-products, the exhaust would contain only water vapor and carbon dioxide. Carbon dioxide (CO_2) isn't directly harmful to health, at least not in low concentrations. After all, CO_2 is also what we exhale after "burning" the calories in the food we eat. However, CO_2 from fossil fuels like gasoline and diesel is very harmful to the environment because it causes global warming—more on this pollutant shortly.

Motor fuel is itself a product and so, like a car, environmental damage occurs throughout its lifecycle as well. For gasoline and diesel, the product lifecycle begins at the oil well and ends when the fuel is burned in the engine. *Fuel cycle* impacts are the forms of pollution and other environmental damage that occur between the oil well and the fuel tank. Gasoline and diesel fuel are poisonous to humans, plants, and animals, and their vapors are toxic. Other energy sources have their own fuel cycles. With battery-powered electric vehicles, for example, no fuel is burned onboard the vehicle, and so nearly all of the fuel-cycle pollution and energy use occurs at electric power plants and in producing the fuels that run the power plants.

Many of the same air pollutants that spew from vehicle tailpipes are also spewed from power plants and oil refineries (as well as the tanker trucks that deliver gasoline to your local filling station).

Gasoline and diesel fuel now provide 97 percent of America's transportation energy needs. Air pollution isn't the only problem associated with these petroleum-based fuels. Oil extraction lays waste to many fragile ecosystems, harming tropical forests in South America and Southeast Asia, deserts and wetlands in the Middle East, our own coastal areas, and the fragile tundra and arctic coastal plains of Alaska. Millions of gallons of oil are spilled every year. Sometimes the disasters are well known, such as the 1989 Exxon Valdez spill in Prince William Sound. More often there are rarely reported but still tragic smaller spills that occur in the oceans and in coastal waters, bays, and rivers throughout the world. In our own communities, groundwater is sometimes tainted by leaks from underground fuel storage tanks and miscellaneous spills that occur during shipping and handling of the 120 billion gallons of fuel we use each year.

In addition to these environmental harms, gasoline and diesel consumption bring economic and security risks. The Middle East contains the largest concentration of the world's oil. The United States maintains a global military presence partly to maintain access to foreign oil. The 1991 war with Iraq was directly related to securing our oil supply. The tragic situation in which the United States finds itself since September 11, 2001, presents many grave challenges for national defense and security. Choosing more fuel-efficient vehicles to reduce our reliance on a world oil market in which Middle Eastern countries play a dominant role is one way we, as individuals, can assist in energy-related aspects of national security.

Major recessions were triggered by oil crises in the 1970s and early 1980s, causing unemployment and inflation. Oil imports drain over $50 billion per year from American pockets, representing lost job opportunities even when our economy seems to be doing fine. Half of U.S. oil is now imported and our dependence on foreign sources is steadily rising, perpetuating the risk of future oil crises. The gasoline price run-ups of the past two years are just the latest examples of how petroleum dependence can squeeze family budgets only to enrich oil producers.

Our addiction to gasoline and diesel fuel also involves moral compromises. It entails deals and economic arrangements with some oil-rich countries whose standards of human rights and environmental protection may not be the same as what we expect at home. Of course, these issues go beyond strictly environmental concerns. Nevertheless, choosing greener vehicles that consume less fuel not only protects the environment, but also helps protect U.S. jobs while reducing the economic costs and moral liabilities of oil dependence.

Major Pollutants Associated with Automobiles

Our focus in the *ACEEE's Green Book™* is on air pollutants related to car and truck fuel consumption, because they are such a large part of a vehicle's environmental damage and because they are the main impacts that can be reduced through your choice of make and model. The adjoining figure shows the amounts of major air pollutants caused by the average new passenger car and light truck in a year. The pollution coming from vehicles can differ depending on the standards they meet (and how well their emissions controls work), how they are driven and maintained, and the quantity and quality of the fuel they burn. Many vans, pickups, sport utilities, and other light trucks meet less stringent emissions and fuel economy standards than vehicles classified as passenger cars. As a result, and as the ratings in this guide indicate, the average light truck pollutes more than the average car.

All new vehicles must meet either the emissions standards set by the U.S. Environmental Protection Agency (EPA) or those set by the California Air Resources Board (CARB). Generally, California standards are more stringent than the Federal standards. A number of Northeastern states have adopted the California standards, and vehicles meeting these stricter standards are now commonly available nationwide.

Vehicles are also tested for fuel economy, as measured by miles per gallon—MPG. Fuel economy standards apply to manufacturers, rather than individual vehicles, and are set so that an automaker can sell a variety of vehicles as long as the average MPG of its sales meets the applicable standard. Manufacturers calculate the fuel economy of each model they sell using laboratory tests similar to those conducted to determine tailpipe emissions. Because these tests give fuel economy estimates higher than what most people experience in real-world driving, the MPG measurements are adjusted downward by EPA. These adjusted MPG numbers are printed on new vehicle stickers and listed here in *ACEEE's Green Book™*.

Although a wide variety of pollutants are formed in the various stages of an automobile's lifecycle, our ratings are mainly based on the serious air pollutants that are regulated to control vehicle emis-

POLLUTION FROM A TYPICAL NEW CAR AND LIGHT TRUCK

Pounds of pollutant per year, including both tailpipe and fuel-cycle emissions and assuming it is driven 15,000 miles per year.

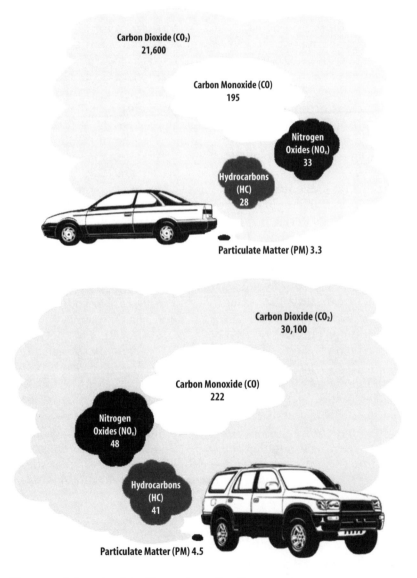

Carbon Dioxide (CO_2)
21,600

Carbon Monoxide (CO)
195

Nitrogen Oxides (NO_x)
33

Hydrocarbons (HC)
28

Particulate Matter (PM) 3.3

Carbon Dioxide (CO_2)
30,100

Carbon Monoxide (CO)
222

Nitrogen Oxides (NO_x)
48

Hydrocarbons (HC)
41

Particulate Matter (PM) 4.5

The average light truck pollutes 40 percent more than the average car.

sions. All of these pollutants are more damaging to health when emitted from vehicle tailpipes than when a similar quantity is emitted from a power plant, since tailpipe pollution is literally "in your face," subjecting people to more direct exposures during daily activities.

Particulate Matter (PM)

Fine airborne particles are an established cause of lung problems, from shortness of breath to worsening of respiratory and cardiovascular disease, damage to lung tissues, and cancer. Certain people are particularly vulnerable to breathing air polluted by fine particles, among them asthmatics, individuals with the flu and with chronic heart or lung diseases, as well as children and the elderly. PM also soils and damages buildings and materials. It forms haze that obscures visibility in many regions. Soot and smoke coming from exhaust pipes are obvious sources of PM, but among the most deadly forms of airborne particulate matter are the invisible fine particles that lodge deeply in the lungs. PM has been regulated for some time, but the regulations were based on counting all particles up to 10 microns in size (PM_{10}). However, PM_{10} standards fail to adequately control the most dangerous, very fine particles. The U.S. EPA has recently started to regulate fine particles up to 2.5 microns in size ($PM_{2.5}$), which better focuses on the most damaging category.

Properly functioning new, fuel-injected gasoline vehicles directly emit very little $PM_{2.5}$. But they indirectly cause significant PM pollution as a result of their NO_x, SO_2, and HC emissions, not only from tailpipes but also from vehicle manufacturing and fuel refining (see below). These emissions result in "secondary" particle formation. This phenomenon refers to the way that the gaseous pollutants agglomerate ("glom up") at microscopic scales to form fine particles that are largely invisible but cause the health problems mentioned. Transportation sources account for about 20 percent of directly emitted $PM_{2.5}$. Diesel engines are the major source of direct PM emissions from motor vehicles. Although most such emissions come from heavy trucks and diesel buses, even the smaller diesel engines in some cars and light trucks emit significant amounts of fine PM.

Nitrogen Oxides (NO_x)

NO_x refers mainly to two chemicals, nitrogen oxide (NO) and nitrogen dioxide (NO_2), that are formed when nitrogen gas, which comprises 78 percent of air, reacts with oxygen during the high temperatures that occur during fuel combustion. NO_x is truly a noxious pollutant in many ways. It is directly hazardous, an irritant to the lungs that can aggravate respiratory problems. It reacts with organic compounds in the air to cause ozone, which is the main reason for "smog alerts" that still happen too often in many cities and regions. NO_x is a precursor of fine particles, which cause respiratory problems and lead to thousands of premature deaths each year. It is also a precursor of acid rain, which harms lakes, waterways, forests, and other ecosystems, as well as damaging buildings and crops. Airborne NO_x also contributes to nitrification—essentially an over-fertilization—of wetlands and bays, leading to algae blooms and fish kills.

As an air pollutant, NO_x is one of the most difficult to control since it is such a pervasive product of combustion. Nationwide, most NO_x comes from electric power plants and industrial sources. Natural gas and oil-fired home furnaces and water heaters also produce NO_x in their flue gases. Motor vehicles account for about one-third of nationwide NO_x emissions. Many of these emissions come from heavy-duty diesel trucks, but cars and light trucks are also a major source. NO_x has also been one of the most difficult pollutants to get out of our air. EPA air quality regulations have helped keep emissions from growing as fast as they might have, but we are not yet making progress in reducing NO_x overall. Despite reduction efforts, NO_x emissions nationwide are 3 percent higher than they were a decade ago. Much of this pollution can be attributed to cars and light trucks.

Sulfur Dioxide (SO_2)

Gasoline and diesel fuels also contain varying amounts of sulfur, which burns in the engine to produce sulfur dioxide (SO_2). This gaseous chemical is another source of secondary particulate formation, and is itself a lung irritant as well as a cause of acid rain. SO_2 also interferes with the operation of catalytic converters. Some of the cleaner, reformulated versions of gasoline have very low sulfur levels. Most gasoline sold nationwide still has too much sulfur, but levels are being reduced under recently established EPA regulations.

Cars and light trucks are not the largest source of SO_2 emissions, which come mainly from power plants and industrial facilities. However, because cars and light trucks are so numerous and gasoline has a high average sulfur content, cars and light trucks cause twice as much fine PM pollution as heavy freight trucks. Making all gasoline as clean as the cleaner, low-sulfur fuels already available in California

Ozone: Helpful in the Stratosphere, But Harmful in the Air We Breathe

Ozone (O_3) is a highly reactive form of oxygen that occurs naturally in various parts of the atmosphere but gets artificially produced in dangerously high concentrations due to emissions from cars, trucks, and other combustion sources.

Up in the stratosphere, ozone helps protect us from ultraviolet radiation. Loss of this protective ozone layer at high altitudes can lead to increased skin cancer. Such concerns have led to restrictions on ozone-depleting chemicals such as those once found in some spray cans and others that have been phased out of use in refrigerators and air conditioners (including automotive air conditioners).

Down in the lower atmosphere, in the air the we breathe, ozone is a health hazard. It is the main ingredient of the smog that causes pollution alerts in many cities around the country. Ozone produced by pollution at low altitudes is of no help in restoring the protective ozone layer at high altitudes. Inhaling air polluted by ozone damages the lungs, reduces breathing ability, and makes us more susceptible to other respiratory problems. Ozone can be deadly to individuals with asthma and other lung conditions, as well as to people with heart conditions. It is also harmful to both adults and children who are otherwise healthy. The risks of shortness of breath, chest pain, lung congestion, and other symptoms caused by ozone are the reasons why public health officials warn us to stay inside and avoid strenuous exercise on severe air pollution days.

Although cars and trucks do not directly emit ozone, they are a major cause of ozone smog. They add to the amount of HC in the air, and tailpipe NO_x reacts with HC to form ozone. Cities without major industries and power plants still have serious smog problems, mostly caused by pollution from cars, trucks, and vans. Although many U.S. cities are seeing better air quality, we'll have to do better at cutting motor vehicle pollution to ensure progress.

would greatly reduce this PM pollution from all cars and trucks on the road, both new and used.

Hydrocarbons (HC)

Hydrocarbons are a broad class of chemicals containing carbon and hydrogen. Those hydrocarbons that cause various forms of air pollution are also known as volatile organic compounds since they are forms of HC that are either gases or readily evaporate into the air. Many forms of HC are directly hazardous, contributing to what are collectively called "air toxics." These compounds can be directly irritating to the lungs and other tissues and they can also cause cancer, contribute to birth defects, and cause other illnesses. During daylight hours, and particularly during hot summer weather, HC reacts with NO_x to form ozone smog (see box at left). Controlling ozone is one of the major environmental challenges in the United States. Although progress has been made over the past several decades, many cities and regions still have smog alerts when ozone levels get too high.

Gasoline vapor contains a mix of hydrocarbons. Thus, HC pollution is produced whenever we fill our tanks. Some regions have special nozzles on fuel pumps to help trap such vapors. Other HC vapors are released at various stages along the way from the refinery to the filling station. Vapors seep out, even when a car is parked and turned off, due to the imperfect sealing of the fuel tank, pipes and hoses, and other components leading to the engine. HC also comes out of the tailpipe, as a result of incomplete combustion and the less-than-perfect cleanup of exhaust gases by catalytic converters and other vehicle emissions controls. Diesel fuel is less volatile than gasoline, so evaporation is less of a problem. Nevertheless, diesel exhaust still contains many toxic hydrocarbons and other compounds. Overall, transportation is responsible for about 36 percent of man-made HC emissions in the United States.

Toxic Chemicals

Toxic releases are just that—any number of a wide range of chemicals that can cause cancer, birth defects, cardiovascular, respiratory and neurological damage, or other forms of health harm. Many smog-forming hydrocarbons are directly toxic; for example, the benzenes found in gasoline are carcinogens.

Other toxics include solvents and metallic compounds such as lead and chromium. Toxics are released during many industrial activities, and car and truck manufacturing is a significant source. Workers and communities near factories and scrappage facilities are at the highest risk. When vehicles are scrapped, bioaccumulative toxins such as lead, chromium, and mercury make their way into the soil, water, and air where they can last for a long time and build up in our bodies and those of other organisms. Vehicles also emit toxics in use, due to fuel evaporation while pumping gas and while a car sits in the sun, for example, as well as from the tailpipe. Diesel exhaust, in particular, has been implicated as a harmful toxic release.

Toxic emissions from cars and trucks, as well as toxic releases during the production and assembly of vehicles and their components, are controlled by various regulations. Factories and other manufacturing fa-

---

The Kyoto Protocol

In December 1997 the nations of the world met in Kyoto, Japan, and agreed to develop a treaty to control emissions of greenhouse gases that are causing global warming. Known as the Kyoto Protocol, the resulting agreement has been refined and subsequently ratified by all of the leading industrial nations except the United States. The treaty calls for wealthier, developed nations to lead the way in significantly reducing their greenhouse gas emissions by 2008-2012. Greener vehicles will be essential for accomplishing that goal. For further information on government actions needed to address global warming, contact www.climatenetwork.org.

---

cilities are required to report toxic emissions from each site. But controls are far from perfect, and there are many ways in which industry could do a better job of preventing toxic pollution. You can find out the source and amount of toxics that are emitted in your community from the Environmental Defense toxic pollution scorecard at www.scorecard.org.

Carbon Monoxide (CO)

Carbon monoxide is an odorless, colorless, but potentially deadly gas that is created by the incomplete combustion of any carbon-containing fuel, including gasoline and diesel. When inhaled, CO combines with the hemoglobin in our blood, impairing the flow of oxygen to our brain and other parts of the body. We've all heard stories of people being killed by carbon monoxide poisoning, from vehicles in closed garages, during fires, or in homes when indoor CO concentrations are raised by malfunctioning stoves or furnaces. Even if it doesn't cause death, CO exposure can cause permanent damage to the nervous system. At lower concentrations, CO is still harmful, particularly for people with heart disease. In some areas, cars and trucks can create enough CO to cause health risks outdoors.

Large amounts of CO are produced when a vehicle first starts up and its engine is cold. Poorly designed and malfunctioning engines and emission controls systems are also responsible for excess CO pollution. Motor vehicles are responsible for about 60 percent of CO emissions nationwide.

Cars, Trucks, and Global Warming

The gasoline-powered automobile was invented just over 100 years ago, when the industrial revolution was still young. Streams had long been dammed to turn mills, and coal was on its way to wide-spread use—it was already powering steamships and locomotives. But most energy used by humans still came from traditional fuels such as wood. In 1890, the world population was about 1.5 billion but growing

GLOBAL CO_2 EMISSIONS: U.S. CARS AND TRUCKS vs. NATIONS OF THE WORLD

Energy-related CO_2 emissions from countries having a 1 percent or greater share of the world total compared with CO_2 emissions from U.S. light duty vehicles (LDVs).

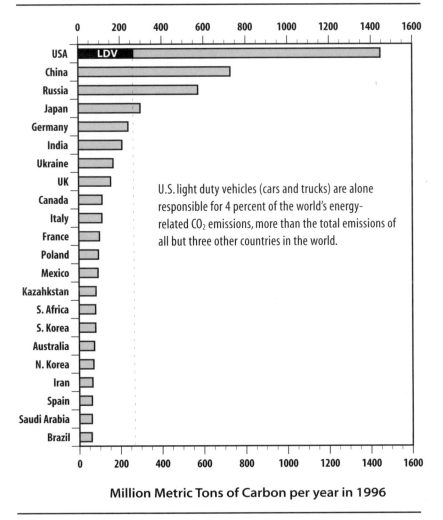

U.S. light duty vehicles (cars and trucks) are alone responsible for 4 percent of the world's energy-related CO_2 emissions, more than the total emissions of all but three other countries in the world.

Million Metric Tons of Carbon per year in 1996

rapidly. The amount of carbon dioxide (CO_2) in the atmosphere was just over 290 parts per million, not yet noticeably over its level throughout pre-industrial civilization.

The world population has now topped six billion and is still growing rapidly. During the past century, the amount of fossil fuel we consume has risen nearly five times faster than population. As a result, the amount of CO_2 in the atmosphere is now over 360 parts per million and climbing. This rapid increase in CO_2 concentration represents the enormous impact of our energy-consumptive lifestyle on the planet, and it is causing dangerous changes to the earth's climate. The past decade has already seen many years with above-normal temperatures. The changes in weather patterns and increases in severe events are consistent with climate disruption. Recent years have been among the warmest ever recorded.

Carbon dioxide is the most important of what are known as greenhouse gases, compounds that enable the earth's atmosphere to trap heat, like a greenhouse, but on a global scale. Too much greenhouse gas in the atmosphere causes global warming, an increase in global average temperatures above what they normally would be.

The risks of global warming are many. Human health is threatened by more frequent and severe heat waves and the spread of tropical diseases. Lives can be lost because of rising sea levels and more severe storms, which can also damage regional and national economies. The disruptions to climate are unpredictable but certainly risky. While some areas may see greater coastal flooding and inundating rains, other regions may experience droughts. Both agriculture and natural habitats can be harmed. Future generations will bear the brunt of these risks, but the effects of global warming have already been detected. Although we cannot attribute any given event to climate change, the increased risks have created a call for action to curtail CO_2 emissions around the world.

Oil is now the world's dominant fuel. There are over 600 million cars and trucks in the world. Both here and abroad, transportation accounts for most oil use. In the United States, we now have more motor vehicles than licensed drivers, and we travel over 2 trillion miles per year, burning 120 billion gallons of gasoline. Not counting the "upstream" emissions from producing the fuel, the result is over a billion tons of CO_2 pollution each year.

U.S. cars and light trucks alone account for more energy-related CO_2 than the nationwide emissions of all but three other countries in the world (China, Russia, and Japan). Our vehicles produce more CO_2 than all of India, which has more than triple our population. U.S. cars and trucks emit twice as much fossil-fuel CO_2 as the economies of either South Korea or Mexico and over three times as much as the whole of

Brazil. Although some of these countries are growing and industrializing rapidly, it will be decades before their level of CO_2 pollution per person approaches ours.

Fuel Economy and Air Pollution

The amount of CO_2 emitted by a vehicle is essentially proportional to the amount of fuel burned. Thus, fuel-efficient vehicles are the best choice for helping to stop global warming. And gas guzzlers are global polluters.

For other forms of air pollution, the relation between fuel economy and emissions is more complex. Automobile emissions are regulated to a given number of grams per mile, independently of a vehicle's fuel economy, but standards are weaker for many gas-guzzling light trucks. Moreover, several factors cause NO_x, HC, CO, and PM pollution to be higher when a vehicle's fuel economy is lower.

In real-world use, most vehicles' emissions are much higher than the standards levels. The reasons include the fact that automakers' and EPA's emissions tests fail to fully represent real-world driving, malfunction of emissions control systems, deterioration of components, inadequate or incorrect maintenance, and sometimes tampering. A portion of this excess pollution is proportional to a vehicle's rate of fuel consumption. Automobiles that meet a more stringent emissions standard are generally cleaner than those that meet a less stringent standard. However, among vehicles that meet the same standard, those with higher fuel economy generally produce less air pollution.

A significant amount of pollution also occurs in supplying vehicles with fuel. These so-called *upstream* emissions occur everywhere from the oil well and refinery to the filling station and gas tank, before the fuel gets to the engine. The relationship between fuel consumption and upstream emissions is strongest for hydrocarbons (HC). For an average car, about 11 grams of excess HC pollution (beyond what comes out of the tailpipe) occurs for every gallon of gasoline burned. Lesser but still-significant amounts of other pollutants are also related to the amount of fuel burned. Examples include NO_x and PM from tanker trucks delivering gasoline and a whole soup of pollutants from oil refineries. Thus, higher fuel consumption implies higher upstream pollution.

Efficiency and Safety

Other things being equal, a smaller, lighter vehicle is more fuel efficient and less polluting than a larger, heavier vehicle. But are smaller, lighter vehicles less safe? The answer is more complex than one might think. In a two-car collision, occupants of the heavier vehicle are typically subjected to lower crash forces. However, the heavier vehicle generally inflicts higher forces on the occupants of the lighter vehicle. Thus, while individuals may gain a measure of protection by driving heavier vehicles, they do so at others' expense. In and of itself, weight does not improve overall safety. Any type of vehicle, including a small car, can be safe when it has well-designed features that improve occupant protection (such as stable, energy-absorbing structures), and properly used occupant restraints (like seat belts, air bags, and child safety seats).

Many of these safety-enhancing features are reflected in crash-test scores and the related safety ratings published by National Highway Traffic Safety Administration (NHTSA) and several consumer publications which we list at the end of this section. These safety ratings are particularly helpful for identifying vehicles that have superior structures, since such features are engineered into a vehicle and are not obvious based on size, shape, or body style.

Better vehicle structures absorb crash energy, cushioning occupants from the severity of an impact. Well-designed structures also act as a "safety cage" that protects occupants from being crushed or otherwise injured by intruding parts of a crashing vehicle. Seat belts protect occupants from striking the inside parts of a vehicle or being thrown out of it. Using seat belts doubles the chance of surviving a serious crash in any vehicle, and air bags further enhance that protection. Improved stability lowers the risk of rollover, a form of accident associated with high fatalities and serious injuries. All of these design features improve safety without adverse trade-offs.

Large and heavy personal vehicles are a mixed bag when it comes to safety. For one thing, heavier vehicles are a greater menace to others on the road: including pedestrians, bicyclists, motorcyclists and occupants of smaller vehicles. Sport Utility Vehicles (SUVs) illustrate the fallacy of "larger is safer" simplistic thinking. While SUVs are heavier on average than passenger cars, they don't necessarily have lower fatality rates. Not only are SUVs more hazardous to others on the road, they threaten their own occupants with higher rollover risks. Many SUVs are less stable than passenger cars and provide poor occupant protection in rollovers. Pickup trucks have the same safety deficiencies as SUVs and many vans are only moderately better. Newer "crossover" body styles, such as all-wheel-drive wagons and sport wagons, reduce some of the safety liabilities of traditional SUVs. In general, because they are detrimental to both safety and the environment, consumers are well advised to avoid SUVs unless they truly have an ongoing need for their larger power, capacity, or off-road ability.

The best guidance is to check the safety ratings as well as the Green Scores of models that you are considering, so that you can find the safest and greenest vehicle that meets your needs. The government safety ratings measure how well a car or truck protects its occupants in various crash tests; recently added rollover ratings indicate how stable a vehicle is. The ratings do not tell the whole story about vehicle safety, since they fail to account for how harmful a vehicle is to others on the road and how well it protects its own occupants in a rollover crash. Nevertheless, crash-test scores are a good comparison of the relative safety of vehicles within a given size class. Look for the "Buying a Safer Car" feature on NHTSA's website (www.nhtsa.dot.gov). Additional advice, information on crashworthiness, and descriptions of safety features by make and model are provided by *The Ultimate Car Book* and *Consumer Reports*.

For Further Information

$\mathbb{C}$heck out *ACEEE's Green Book*™ website at **GreenerCars.com** for up-dated Green Scores and other information on new vehicles as they come on the market. Here is a list of organizations and Web sites providing additional information on the environmental impact of automobiles and ways to reduce it.

Clean Car Campaign

The Clean Car Campaign is a collaboration by ACEEE and allied organizations working to promote a greening of the automobile industry. We are asking automakers to design cars and trucks that are progressively less harmful to the environment during production, use, and scrappage.

Take the "Clean Car Pledge" by promising to buy the greenest vehicle that meets your needs and fits your budget, and asking automakers to offer products that achieve a Clean Car Standard for high efficiency, low emissions, and clean production: **www.CleanCarCampaign.org**.

Government Agencies

- The *Fuel Economy Guide* published by the U.S. Department of Energy and the U.S. Environmental Protection Agency, www.fueleconomy.gov

- California Air Resources Board, Buyer's Guide to Cleaner Cars, www.arb.ca.gov/msprog/ccbg/ccbg.htm

- U.S. Department of Energy Clean Cities Program, www.ccities.doe.gov

- U.S. Department of Energy Office of Transportation Technologies, "Facts and Analysis" page, www.ott.doe.gov/facts.html

- National Highway Traffic Safety Administration, www.nhtsa.dot.gov

Public Interest Organizations

■ American Council for an Energy-Efficient Economy
1001 Connecticut Avenue, N.W., Suite 801
Washington, DC 20036
www.aceee.org

■ Center For Auto Safety
1825 Connecticut Avenue, NW, Suite 330
Washington, DC 20009-5708
www.autosafety.org

■ The Ecology Center
117 North Division Street
Ann Arbor, MI 48104
www.ecocenter.org/auto.html

■ Environmental Defense
1875 Connecticut Avenue, N.W., Sixth Floor
Washington, DC 20009
www.environmentaldefense.org

■ Natural Resources Defense Council
40 West 20th Street
New York, NY 10011
www.nrdc.org/air/transportation

■ Public Citizen
1600 20th Street, N.W.
Washington, DC 20009
www.citizen.org

■ Sierra Club
85 Second Street, Second Floor
San Francisco, CA 94105-3441
www.sierraclub.org

■ Union of Concerned Scientists
Two Brattle Square
PO Box 9105
Cambridge, MA 02238-9105
www.ucsusa.org/transportation

Other Consumer Resources

- *The Ultimate Car Book* by Jack Gillis

- The Consumer Reports *New Car Yearbook.* See also the Consumers Union Web site: www.ConsumerReports.org

- EVWorld.com—online news about electric and other advanced vehicles

- MyWorld.com—web portal containing many environmental information resources, including automotive pages based on *ACEEE's Green Book*™.

Appendix:
How the Ratings Are Calculated

Many factors determine the environmental impact of a car or light truck. Tailpipe emissions and fuel efficiency are clearly important, but impacts also depend on the type of fuel used and the materials that go into manufacturing the vehicle. A scientific approach for estimating the environmental impacts of a product is known as *lifecycle assessment*, since it traces the impacts of a product from "cradle to grave": materials production and product manufacturing; emissions and other effects when the product is in use; through end-of-life effects of disposal and recycling. We developed the Green Scores and Class Rankings according to the principles of lifecycle assessment, using available data that are sufficiently standardized to be applicable to all makes and models.

Three types of vehicle-specific data form the basis of the *ACEEE's Green Book* ratings: tailpipe emissions, given by the emissions standard to which a vehicle is certified; fuel economy, based on EPA test cycles; and vehicle mass (curb weight).

In real-world driving, tailpipe pollution (CO, HC, NO_x, and PM) can be as much as 3 times higher than the nominal grams-per-mile (g/mi) emission standard to which a vehicle is certified. These excess emissions occur for a variety of reasons: inaccuracy of the tests, malfunctioning emission control systems; and deterioration of the catalytic converter and other components. Therefore, we apply adjustment factors, similar to those used in EPA's vehicle emissions calculation models, to determine the expected lifetime average emissions for vehicles meeting a given standard. The same adjustment factors are used for all makes and models certifying to a given emissions standard for a given fuel. Our adjustment factors reflect emission reductions based on EPA's recent improvements to the tests that automakers must use to certify their vehicles.

Fuel economy data are used to calculate greenhouse gas emissions, fuel-cycle criteria emissions (air pollution due to producing and distributing the fuel), and those aspects of vehicle emissions that are related to fuel consumption rates (such as a portion of evaporative HC emissions). Fuel economy determines a vehicle's energy consumption rate (gallons/mile, or kWh/mile or Btu/mile for electric and alternative-fueled vehicles). This value is multiplied by national average emission factors for the various pollutants to give emission rates in grams per mile. The greenhouse gas emissions portion of these results is shown in our Green Ratings master tables as the GHG number, given in tons per year.

Vehicle weight is used as the basis for estimating manufacturing impacts. Standardized, model-specific data on the environmental damage of vehicle manufacturing are not available. Therefore we use average manufacturing-sector emission factors and average breakdowns of vehicle materials by weight. These statistics determine the average emissions of each pollutant per unit of vehicle weight, which are multiplied by vehicle weight and divided by average vehicle lifetime mileage to estimate emissions related to manufacturing. We did not have sufficient data to estimate vehicle disposal and scrappage impacts, but these impacts are much smaller than manufacturing and in-use impacts, and, in general, would also be proportional to vehicle weight. For electric vehicles, we account for the weight of the replacement batteries needed over the vehicle's lifetime.

Having determined the average emission rates for each major stage of the vehicle's lifecycle (including those associated with the fuel consumed), the next step is to determine the relative environmental damage done by each pollutant. An economics-based approach for assessing environmental harm involves estimates of *damage costs* associated with a given pollutant. Specified, for example, in cents per gram ($\textcent/g$) of pollutant, these estimates reflect the costs to society of illnesses and premature deaths associated with pollution. Damage cost estimation involves uncertainties, of course, but it may also fail to reflect the full value we place on our health, environmental quality, and the protection of ecosystems. In spite of these limitations, damage costs provide a rational and consistent way to account for the different effects of various pollutants, and so we apply them to the emissions rates calculated from the vehicle data.

It is very difficult to estimate a damage cost for CO_2 and other greenhouse gases. The damage due to global warming is just beginning to occur and the worst risks are largely in the future. Therefore, we cannot look back at the harm that has already occurred—as has been done for conventionally regulated pollutants such as NO_x and PM—in order to estimate damage costs. However, because of the grave risks and growing concerns about greenhouse gas emissions, we give global warming concerns equal weight to other forms of air pollution in determining our green vehicle ratings. Therefore, we assigned CO_2 emissions a cost value such that, for the average 2002 light duty vehicle, half of the overall environmental harm is associated with global warming risks and the other half is associated with the health effects of conventional air pollutants.

Multiplying the gram-per-mile pollutant rates by their appropriate cents-per-gram damage costs (which vary by pollutant and location of emissions) yields environmental impact estimates in cents per mile (¢/mi). For conventionally regulated pollutants, adding these estimates up for a typical year of driving results in the "Health Cost" number shown in the main tables.

Adding up the ¢/mi estimates for all pollutants, including greenhouse gases, gives a total impact estimate for a given vehicle, which we term its *environmental damage index* (EDX). The EDX is the main result of our analysis for each vehicle and it provides the common metric with which we compare different makes and models. The EDX represents environmental harm; thus, the lower the EDX, the greener the vehicle.

For a green scoring system, greener vehicles should get higher scores. Therefore, we converted the EDX to a Green Score on a scale of 0–100 by grading along a curve, using a formula specified so that an EDX of zero corresponds to a Green Score of 100.

Finally, to determine the class ranking symbols, we examined the range of EDX values within each vehicle class. Cutpoints were determined on the basis of the distribution unique to each class. In addition, for a model to earn a "superior" class rating (✔), its Green Score must be better than the overall average Green Score, as well as being among the highest in its class. This year, the overall average EDX is 2.42¢/mi, corresponding to a Green Score of 22. The average car has a Green Score of 29 and the average light truck has a Green Score of 19.

Further information on the analysis behind the ratings may be obtained by ordering our technical report, *Rating the Environmental Impacts of Motor Vehicles: ACEEE's Green Book™ Methololology*, available from ACEEE publications.

List of Acronyms

Throughout the *Green Book* we've introduced and used a variety of acronyms and abbreviations. They are listed here along with their definitions to make it easier to follow the text.

ACEEE   American Council for an Energy-Efficient Economy

Btu   British thermal unit: a measure of energy

CARB   California Air Resources Board

CO   Carbon monoxide: a hazardous tailpipe pollutant

CO_2 Carbon dioxide: a product of fuel combustion and the principal greenhouse gas that causes global warming

DOE   U.S. Department of Energy

EDX   Environmental damage index

EPA   U.S. Environmental Protection Agency

FFV   Flexible Fuel Vehicle

GHG   Greenhouse gas: causes global warming

HC   Hydrocarbon: toxic and ozone-forming pollutant

kWh   kilowatt-hour: a measure of electrical energy

LEV   Low-Emission Vehicle

MPG   Miles per gallon: a measure of fuel economy

NHTSA   National Highway Traffic Safety Administration

NO_x Nitrogen oxides: pollutant of multiple hazards

SO_2 Sulfur dioxide: pollutant of multiple hazards

SULEV   Super-Ultra-Low-Emission Vehicle

Tier 1   Principal Federal emission standard since 1994

TLEV   Transitional Low-Emission Vehicle

ULEV   Ultra-Low-Emission Vehicle

ZEV   Zero-Emission Vehicle

Alphabetical Vehicle Index

ACURA
3.2CL 73
3.2CL Type-S 73
3.2TL 82
3.5RL 82
MDX 102
NSX 66
RSX 68

ASTON MARTIN
Vanquish 66

AUDI
A4 .73
A4 Quattro 73
A6 .82
A6 Avant Quattro 87
A6 Quattro 82
A8 L 88
A8 Quattro 82
Allroad Quattro 87
S4 .73
S4 Avant 80
S6 Avant 87
S8 Quattro 82
TT Coupe 68
TT Coupe Quattro 68
TT Roadster 66
TT Roadster Quattro 66

BENTLEY
Arnage 82
Arnage LWB 88
Azure 68

BENTLEY (cont.)
Continental R 73
Continental SC 68
Continental T 68

BMW
325Ci 68
325Ci Convertible 68
325i 73
325i Sport Wagon 80
325xi 73
325xi Sport Wagon 80
330Ci 68
330Ci Convertible 68
330i 73
330xi 73
525i 73
525i Sport Wagon 80
530i 74
540i 74
540i Sport Wagon 80
745i 88
745Li 88
M Coupe 66
M Roadster 66
M3 68
M3 Convertible 68
M5 74
X5 3.0i 102
X5 4.4i 102
X5 4.6is 102
Z3 Coupe 66
Z3 Roadster 66
Z8 .66

BUICK
Century 82
LeSabre 89
Park Avenue 89
Regal 82
Rendezvous 103

CADILLAC
Deville 89
Eldorado 82
Escalade 107
Escalade EXT 107
Limousine 89
Seville 82

CHEVROLET
Astro (Cargo) 90
Astro (Passenger) 90
Avalanche 97
Blazer 103
Camaro 69
Cavalier 74
Corvette 66
G1500/2500 Express 92
G1500/2500 Van 92
Impala 89
Malibu 82
Monte Carlo 83
Prizm 74
S-10 94
Silverado C1500 97
Silverado K1500 97
Silverado K2500 97
Suburban C1500 107
Suburban K1500 107
Suburban K2500 107
Tahoe C1500 107
Tahoe K1500 107
Tracker Convertible 99
Tracker Hardtop 99
Tracker LT 100
Tracker ZR2 100
Tracker ZR2 Convertible . .100

CHEVROLET (cont.)
Trailblazer 103
Venture 91

CHRYSLER
300M 89
Concorde 89
Prowler 66
PT Cruiser 80
Sebring Convertible 74
Sebring Coupe 74
Sebring Sedan 83
Town & Country 91
Voyager 91

DAEWOO
Lanos 74
Leganza 83
Nubira 75
Nubira Wagon 80

DODGE
Caravan 91
Dakota 94
Durango 103
Intrepid 89
Neon 75
Ram Pickup 1500 97
Ram Pickup 2500 98
Ram Van 1500 93
Ram Van 2500 93
Ram Wagon 1500 93
Ram Wagon 2500 93
Stratus Coupe 75
Stratus Sedan 83

FERRARI
360 Modena/Spider 66

FORD
Crown Victoria 89
E-150 Club Wagon 93
E-150 Econoline 93

FORD (cont.)
E-250 Econoline 93
Escape 100
Escort 75
Escort ZX2 69
Excursion 107
Expedition 107
Explorer 103
Explorer Sport 104
Explorer Sport Trac 95
F-150 98
F-250 Super Duty 98
Focus 75
Focus Wagon 87
Mustang 69
Ranger 95
Taurus 89
Taurus Wagon 87
Thunderbird 66
Windstar Van 91
Windstar Wagon 91

GMC
Envoy 104
G1500/2500 Savana
(Cargo) 94
G1500/2500 Savana
(Passenger) 94
Jimmy 104
Safari (Cargo) 91
Safari (Passenger) 91
Sierra C1500 98
Sierra Denali 98
Sierra K1500 99
Sierra K2500 99
Sonoma 95
Yukon C1500 108
Yukon Denali 108
Yukon K1500 108
Yukon XL C1500 108
Yukon XL Denali 108
Yukon XL K1500 108
Yukon XL K2500 108

HONDA
Accord 83
Civic 75
Civic GX 75
Civic HX 69
CR-V 100
Insight 67
Odyssey 91
Passport 104
S2000 67

HYUNDAI
Accent 75
Elantra 76
Santa Fe 100
Sonata 83
XG350 83

INFINITI
G20 76
I35 83
Q45 84
QX4 104

ISUZU
Axiom 104
Hombre 95
Rodeo 104
Rodeo Sport 100
Trooper 104

JAGUAR
S-Type 84
Super V8 84
Vanden Plas 84
X-Type 76
XJ Sport 76
XJ8 76
XJR 76
XK8 69
XK8 Convertible 69
XKR 69
XKR Convertible 69

JEEP
Grand Cherokee 105
Liberty 100
Wrangler 100

KIA
Optima 84
Rio 76
Sedona 92
Spectra 76
Sportage 101

LAMBORGHINI
L-147 Murcielago 67

LAND ROVER
Discovery Series II 105
Freelander 101
Range Rover 108

LEXUS
ES 300 84
GS 300 84
GS 430 84
IS 300 76
LS 430 84
LX 470 108
RX 300 101
SC 430 69

LINCOLN
Blackwood 99
Continental 90
LS 84
Navigator 108
Town Car 90

MAZDA
626 84
B2300 95
B3000 96
B4000 96
Millenia 76
MPV 92

MAZDA (cont.)
MX-5 Miata 67
Protege/Protege5 76
Tribute 101

MERCEDES-BENZ
C230 Kompressor 77
C240 77
C32 AMG 77
C320 77
C320 Wagon 81
CL500 77
CL55 AMG 77
CL600 77
CLK320 69
CLK320 Cabriolet 69
CLK430 70
CLK430 Cabriolet 70
CLK55 AMG 70
CLK55 AMG Cabriolet 70
E320 85
E320 4matic 85
E320 4matic Wagon 87
E320 Wagon 87
E430 85
E430 4matic 85
E55 AMG 85
G500 105
ML320 105
ML500 105
ML55 AMG 105
S430 90
S500 90
S55 AMG 90
S600 90
SL500 67
SL600 67
SLK230 Kompressor 67
SLK32 AMG 67
SLK320 67

MERCURY
Cougar 77
Grand Marquis 90

MERCURY (cont.)
Mountaineer 105
Sable 85
Sable Wagon 87
Villager 92

MITSUBISHI
Diamante 85
Eclipse 70
Eclipse Spyder 70
Galant 85
Lancer 77
Mirage 70
Montero 105
Montero Sport 105

NISSAN
Altima 85
Frontier 96
Maxima 85
Pathfinder 106
Quest 92
Sentra 77
Sentra CA 77
Xterra 106

OLDSMOBILE
Alero 78
Aurora 85
Bravada 106
Intrigue 85
Silhouette 92

PONTIAC
Aztek 106
Bonneville 90
Firebird 70
Grand Am 78
Grand Prix 86
Montana 92
Sunfire 78

PORSCHE
911 Carrera 70
911 Carrera 4 Cabriolet 70

PORSCHE (cont.)
911 Carrera 4S 71
911 Carrera Cabriolet 71
911 GT2 67
911 Targa 71
911 Turbo 71
Boxster 67
Boxster S 67

ROLLS-ROYCE
Corniche 71
Park Ward 90
Silver Seraph 86

SAAB
9-3 .86
9-3 Convertible 71
9-3 Viggen 86
9-3 Viggen Convertible 71
9-5 .86
9-5 Wagon 87

SATURN
L100/200 86
L300 86
LW200 87
LW300 87
SC .71
SL .78
VUE 101

SUBARU
Forester 101
Impreza 2.5 RS Sedan 71
Impreza 2.5 TS Sport
Wagon 81
Impreza Outback Sport . . .81
Impreza WRX Sedan 71
Impreza WRX Sport
Wagon 81
Legacy Sedan 78
Legacy Wagon 88
Outback Sedan 78
Outback Wagon 88

SUZUKI

Esteem 71
Esteem Wagon 81
Grand Vitara 101
Grand Vitara XL-7 101
Vitara 2-Door 102
Vitara 4-Door 102

TOYOTA

4Runner 106
Avalon 90
Camry 86
Camry Solara 78
Camry Solara Convertible .72
Celica 72
Corolla 78
Echo 79
Highlander 106
Land Cruiser 109
MR2 67
Prius 79
RAV4 102
Sequoia 109
Sienna 92
Tacoma 96
Tundra 99

VOLKSWAGEN

Cabrio 72
Eurovan 94
Eurovan Camper 94
Golf 79
GTI 79
Jetta 79
Jetta Wagon 81
New Beetle 72
Passat 86
Passat 4motion 79
Passat Wagon 88
Passat Wagon 4motion 88

VOLVO

C70 Convertible 72
C70 Coupe 79
Cross Country 88

VOLVO (cont.)

S40 79
S60 80
S80 86
S80 T6/Executive 86
V40 81
V70 88

Bibliography

American Automobile Association. 1997. Gas Saving Tips. Heathrow, FL: American Automobile Association.

Bradsher, K. 1997. A Deadly Highway Mismatch Ignored. *The New York Times*, p. A1, September 24.

Calvert, J.G., J.B. Heywood, R.F. Sawyer, and J.H. Seinfeld. 1993. Achieving Acceptable Air Quality: Some Reflections on Controlling Vehicle Emissions. *Science*, 261, pp. 37–45.

Consumer Reports. 1996. Turning Up the Heat, Special Report on Global Warming and Environment. *Consumer Reports*, pp. 38–44, September.

———. 1997. Clearing the Air: Is Our Air Clean Enough? Special Report on Air Quality. *Consumer Reports*, pp. 36–38, August.

———. 1997. How Safe Are Sport Utility Vehicles? *Consumer Reports*, p. 54, June.

DeCicco, J., and J. Kliesch. 2001. *Rating the Environmental Impacts of Motor Vehicles: ACEEE's Green Book™ Methodology*. Technical Report. Washington, D.C.: American Council for an Energy-Efficient Economy.

DeCicco, J., and M. Ross. 1994. Improving Automotive Efficiency. *Scientific American*, 271 (6), pp. 52–55.

DeCicco, J., and M. Thomas. 1999. A Method for Green Rating of Automobiles. *Journal of Industrial Ecology* 3 (1), pp. 55-75.

Delucchi, M.A. 1991. *Emissions of Greenhouse Gases from the Use of Transportation Fuels and Electricity*. Report ANL/ESD/TM-22. Argonne, Ill.: Argonne National Laboratory, Center for Transportation Research.

———. 1996. *The Annualized Social Costs of Motor Vehicle Use in the U.S., 1990–1991: Summary of Theory, Data, Methods, and Results*. Report 1. Davis, Calif.: Institute of Transportation Studies, University of California.

Dyson, C., B. Magavern, J. Shah, and T. Stephens. 1995. *The Green Buyer's Car Book*. Washington, D.C.: Public Citizen.

Energy Innovations. 1997. *Energy Innovations: A Prosperous Path to a Clean Environment*. Washington, D.C.: Alliance to Save Energy, American Council for an Energy-Efficient Economy, Natural

Resources Defense Council, Tellus Institute, and Union of Concerned Scientists.

Gillis, J. 2000. *The Ultimate Car Book*. New York: Harper Collins.

Greene, D.L. 1997. Economic Scarcity: Forget Geology, Beware Monopoly. In Special Issue, "Running on Empty: Emerging Challenges in Global Energy Security." *Harvard International Review*, XIX (3), pp. 16–19; 65–67, Summer.

Hwang, R. 1997. *Are Cars Still a Problem? Real-World Emission Reductions from Passenger Vehicles over the Past 30 Years*. Berkeley, Calif.: Union of Concerned Scientists.

Keoleian, G., K. Kar, M.M. Manion, and J.W. Buckley. 1997. *Industrial Ecology of the Automobile: A Lifecycle Perspective*. Warrendale, Penn.: Society of Automotive Engineers.

Makower, J. 1992. *The Green Commuter*. Washington, D.C.: National Press Books.

Ross, M., R. Goodwin, R. Watkins, M. Wang, and T. Wenzel. 1995. *Real-World Emissions from Model Year 1993, 2000 and 2010 Passenger Cars*. Washington, D.C.: American Council for an Energy-Efficient Economy.

Seidel, S.R. 1996. Keeping Cars Cool. Chapter 11 in *Ozone Protection in the United States: Elements of Success*. Ed. E. Cook. Washington, D.C.: World Resources Institute.

Shprentz, D.S. 1996. *Breath-Taking: Premature Mortality Due to Particulate Air Pollution in 239 American Cities*. Washington, D.C.: Natural Resources Defense Council.

U.S. Environmental Protection Agency. 1992. *What You Can Do to Reduce Air Pollution*. EPA 450-K-002. Washington, D.C.: EPA.

———. 1994. *Tips to Save Gas and Improve Mileage*. EPA Fact Sheet OMS-17 (EPA 400-F-92-004). Washington, D.C.: EPA.

———. 1994. *Your Car and Clean Air: What You Can Do to Reduce Pollution*. EPA Fact Sheet OMS-18 (EPA 400-F-93-002). Washington, D.C.: EPA.

———. 1995. *National Air Quality and Emissions Trends Report, 1994*. EPA 454-R-95-014. Research Triangle Park, N.C.: EPA.

Yergin, D. 1991. *The Prize: The Epic Quest for Oil, Money, and Power*. New York: Simon and Schuster.

About the Authors

JOHN DECICCO is a Senior Fellow at Environmental Defense and expert on transportation energy use, emissions, and vehicle technology. He conducts research on automotive issues and has published extensively, writing for both popular and technical audiences. As a former Senior Associate at ACEEE, he pioneered *ACEEE's Green Book*™ in order to provide better consumer information on environmental aspects of the automotive marketplace. He also co-edited the book *Transportation, Energy, and Environment: How Far Can Technology Take Us?* and the study *Energy Innovations: A Prosperous Path to a Clean Environment.* He received his Ph.D. in Mechanical Engineering from Princeton University in 1988, where he was affiliated with the University's Center for Energy and Environmental Studies.

JAMES KLIESCH is a transportation analyst at ACEEE, where he conducts research on an array of vehicle- and energy-related topics. His work includes development of the software used for assessing the vehicles in this book, performing CO_2 emissions trend analyses, and co-authoring reports such as *Rating the Environmental Impacts of Motor Vehicles: ACEEE's Green Book Methodology.* In addition to his *Green Book* responsibilities at ACEEE, he is the principal manager of the Greener-Cars.com website. He earned his B.S. in Electrical Engineering from Ohio University, and M.S. in Environmental and Energy Policy from the University of Delaware.

ALSO AVAILABLE FROM ACEEE
Books on Transportation

Transportation, Energy, and Environment: How Far Can Technology Take Us? examines the potential for technological improvements in highway vehicles, railroads, and aircraft to move the U.S. transportation system toward greater sustainability.

Edited by John DeCicco, ACEEE, and Mark Delucchi, Institute of Transportation Studies.

ISBN 0-918249-28-7 • Soft cover, 6"x 9", 278 pp., index, 1997, $33

Transportation and Energy: Strategies for a Sustainable Transportation System analyzes how transportation energy choices made by citizens, policymakers, and planners will affect national goals of mobility, accessibility, environmental quality, economic growth, and energy security.

Edited by Daniel Sperling and Susan A. Shaheen, Institute of Transportation Studies.

ISBN 0-918249-20-1 • Soft cover, 6"x 9", 320 pp., index, 1995, $31

Transportation and Global Climate Change focuses on the transportation sector's role in global warming and what can be done about it.

Edited by David L. Greene, Oak Ridge National Laboratory, and Danilo J. Santini, Argonne National Laboratory.

ISBN 0-918249-17-1 • Soft cover, 6"x 9", 357 pp., index, 1993, $31

Consumer Guides

Consumer Guide to Home Energy Savings

This illustrated, 244-page book contains expanded listings of energy-efficient appliances and practical suggestions on how to reduce energy use and help protect the environment through home improvements. This guide is available in bookstores ($8.95) or directly from ACEEE ($13.95 postpaid).

Guide to Energy-Efficient Commercial Equipment

Using this guide, buyers can specify and select the most energy-efficient commercial equipment—lighting options, space conditioning equipment, and motors for commercial applications. It presents criteria for selecting efficient equipment and lists the most efficient commercial equipment on the market, as well as provides information about how to operate and maintain the equipment. This new edition features a new chapter on selecting other energy-using equipment, such as office equipment ($30.00 postpaid).

For More Information or To Order, contact ACEEE Publications Office
Phone: 202-429-8873 / Fax: 202-429-0193
ace3pubs@ix.netcom.com

Visit ACEEE's World Wide Web homepage at www.aceee.org